MW00980065

The Organic Union in God's Relationship with Man

WITNESS LEE

Living Stream Ministry
Anaheim, California

First Edition, 4,000 copies. October 1993.

ISBN 0-87083-736-2

Published by

Living Stream Ministry
1853 W. Ball Road, Anaheim, CA 92804 U.S.A.
P. O. Box 2121, Anaheim, CA 92814 U.S.A.

Printed in the United States of America

CONTENTS

PREFACE

This book is composed of messages given by Brother Witness Lee in Seattle, Washington on September 3-6, 1993.

Chapter One

IN THE CREATION OF MAN

Scripture Reading: Gen. 1:26a; Col. 1:15a; Gen. 2:7; Prov. 20:27; Job 32:8; Zech. 12:1; John 4:24; 3:6b; 1 Cor. 6:17; Gal. 5:16; Rom. 8:4b; Gen. 2:8-9; Psa. 36:9a; John 1:1-4a; 14:6a; Col. 3:4a; Rev. 2:7; 22:2; Gen. 2:16; John 6:57b; 15:5; Phil. 1:20-21a

OUTLINE

I. In God's image and according to His likeness—Gen. 1:26a:
   A. Not in God's image and according to His likeness merely in form.
   B. But by God's life in an organic union with Him.
   C. Not to produce a toy without life, but to produce a living and genuine manifestation and expression of God with His life.
   D. As Christ being the living image of the invisible God in life—Col. 1:15a.
   E. Thus, the man created by God in His image and according to His likeness must be in the organic union with God.

II. With a spirit created by God—Gen. 2:7:
   A. The breath of life breathed by God into man's body formed with dust—Prov. 20:27; Job 32:8.
   B. This spirit of man is ranked with the heavens and the earth in the holy Word of God—Zech. 12:1:
      1. The heavens are for the earth.
      2. The earth is for man to exist.
      3. The spirit of man is for God:
         a. To worship God—John 4:24.
         b. To be regenerated by God—John 3:6b.

c. To be joined to God—1 Cor. 6:17.
d. That man may walk and live in the organic union with God—Gal. 5:16; Rom. 8:4b.

III. Putting man before the tree of life—Gen. 2:8-9:
A. The tree of life is a figure signifying God as life to man—Psa. 36:9a; John 1:1-4a; 14:6a; Col. 3:4a; Rev. 2:7; 22:2.
B. Good for man to take and eat—Gen. 2:16; John 6:57b.
C. That man may be constituted with God as the constituent of life.
D. Thus, man and God become organically united and live together as one person—John 15:5; Phil. 1:20-21a.

The general subject of this book is the organic union in God's relationship with man. The crucial points in this book can be summarized by the following four sentences:

1) God created man for the purpose that man may take Him as life for man to live Him and express Him.

2) God incarnated Himself to be a man that He might be united with man organically.

3) Christ saves man with His dynamic life that man may be able even to reign in His eternal life.

4) Christ builds up His Body by His believers growing up into Him, as the Head, in all things that His Body may be consummated in the New Jerusalem as the eternal manifestation and expression of the Triune God in His unlimited life.

In the Bible what is unveiled to us is simply the organic union in God's relationship with man. In the six chapters of this book we will cover the six major steps of this organic union, from the first two chapters of the Bible to the last two chapters. The first step of the organic union is God's creation of man. This is fully recorded in the first two chapters of Genesis. At the end of the Bible the organic union in God's relationship with man consummates in the New Jerusalem. This is fully unveiled in the last two chapters of Revelation. Between these two ends are the remaining four steps of the organic union: God's incarnation, God's salvation, the growth of the believers, and the building up of the Body of Christ. These six steps cover the entire Bible and give us the details of this organic union.

THE CREATION OF MAN BY GOD

Most Christians have read through the first two chapters of the Bible concerning God's creation of man. However, most of the students and even the teachers of the Bible have not entered into the intrinsic significance of this portion of the holy Word. The way to study, to understand, and to interpret the holy Word is exemplified by the Lord Jesus in Matthew 22:23-33. One day the Sadducees, who did not believe in the resurrection (v. 23; Acts 23:8), asked the Lord Jesus concerning seven brothers who consecutively and respectively married one woman. They asked the Lord whose wife this woman would be in the resurrection. The Lord answered, "You err, not knowing the Scriptures nor the power of God" (v. 29). In the Lord's answer He told the Sadducees that, although they had the Pentateuch, the Scriptures, in their hands, they did not understand it. Then the Lord quoted Moses' writing in Exodus 3:6: "I am the God of Abraham and the God of Isaac and the God of Jacob" (v. 32). Next, the Lord interpreted His quotation of the holy Word, telling the Sadducees that God is not the God of the dead but of the living. The Lord saw the intrinsic significance of the threefold divine title *the God of Abraham and the God of Isaac and the God of Jacob,* that is, that God is not only the God of Abraham, Isaac, and Jacob, but He is the God of the living. Thus, the Lord used this divine title, with the life and power implied in it, to prove to the Sadducees that the dead Abraham, Isaac, and Jacob will be resurrected. This is the way to interpret the Bible.

After many years of studying Genesis 1 and 2, my conclusion is that in such a wonderful and marvelous record concerning the creation of man by God, there are three striking points. Every one of these points is crucial.

IN GOD'S IMAGE AND ACCORDING TO HIS LIKENESS

The first crucial and striking point concerning God's creation of man is that God created man in His image and according to His likeness (Gen. 1:26a). What is God's image? Since God is invisible, it is difficult to understand how the invisible God could have an image. In Colossians 1:15 we are told that Christ is the image of the invisible God. Still, we may ask what it means to say that Christ is the image of God. We may also wonder what the likeness of God is, and what the difference between image and likeness is. For years I did not understand what God's image and God's likeness are. Gradually, I began to understand that God's image is what God is in His divine attributes. God is love (1 John 4:8); God is light (1:5); God is holy (Lev. 19:2) and is even holiness (Heb. 12:10); and God is righteous (Psa. 7:9b) and is even righteousness (Jer. 23:6). God is also patient and is even patience itself.

One day nearly sixty years ago I went to visit Brother

Watchman Nee at his home. Immediately after sitting down, he raised the question, "Witness, please tell me, what is patience?" I was surprised that he would ask me such a simple question. I thought I knew what patience is. However, since it was Brother Nee who asked me concerning patience, I realized that his question was not simple. Therefore, I did not dare to answer quickly. After considering my response for some time, I said, "Patience is to suffer silently the mistreatment of others." However, Brother Nee replied that that was not patience. Eventually, he said to me, "Patience is Christ." From Brother Nee's response we can realize that patience is God Himself. We are not patient. All of us, young and old, male and female, have lost our temper many times. In a given day we may lose our temper several times. This shows that we have no patience. Patience is not us. Patience is God. Patience is one of the attributes of God.

Only God is all kinds of virtues. God is kindness, forbearance, and even humility. No one is genuinely humble; only God is humble. One day God humbled Himself to become a man. He was God, lofty in the universe; but the great, unlimited God came down to the lowest part of the universe to be a small, limited man. In John 7:6 He told His brothers in the flesh, "My time has not yet come, but your time is always ready." By this He indicated that while He lived here on earth as a man, He, the eternal, infinite, unlimited God, was limited even in the matter of time. This is genuine humility.

We human beings are lacking in genuine virtues. A man and woman may love each other during their courtship, but immediately after their wedding they may argue with each other. It is common for a husband and wife to quarrel and lose their tempers. Only God does not have any temper.

God's image is the totality, the aggregate, of all that He is. He is love, He is light, He is patience, He is kindness, He is mercy, and He is forbearance. All the items of God's attributes added together equal the image of God. When Christ came to express God in humanity, He expressed God in all His attributes. This is God's image. God created man in this image. Therefore, we all have a small amount of love, light, and other virtues. We are not animals; we are human beings created in the image of God. Hence, we do have some virtues, although they are temporal and do not last. God made us as men in His image to express what He is. In this expression God's attributes become our virtues. God's likeness is just the expression of what God is. God's image is what God is. When this image is expressed, that is God's likeness. As human beings we were made in God's image to express what He is. Thus, we were made according to His likeness.

In God's creation we are all made God in the sense that we were created in God's image and according to God's likeness. This means that we all look like God. To be made God in this sense is not to be made an object of worship. We are not God in that sense. We look like God, just as a photograph of a person looks like the person, because we were made in God's image and according to His likeness. When we say that we look like God, it may seem that we are deifying ourselves. If we do not look like God, whom do we look like? Yes, it is true that we look like man. However, in whose image and according to whose likeness was man made? Man was made in the image of God and according to the likeness of God. Therefore, man was created after God's kind. In Genesis 1 we are told that in God's creation, God made the plants and the animals after their own kind, respectively (vv. 12, 21, 24-25). However, man, who was created in the image and likeness of God, was made after God's kind, not man's kind. Therefore, at least we can say that we are like God.

God did not create man in His image and according to His likeness merely in form. Toy makers make toys in human form, but in that form there is no reality, because there is no life within the toys. God created man in His image and according to His likeness not only in form but also in life in order that man could be one with God in nature and in life. God's intention in creating man was that God and man, man and God, could be joined in a union that is altogether organic, in life. This organic union is by God's life. In His creation of man, God did not produce a toy without life, but He produced man as a living and genuine manifestation and expression of God with His life, just as Christ is the living image of the invisible God in life. Thus, the man created by God in His image and according to His likeness must be in the organic union with God.

WITH A SPIRIT CREATED BY GOD

The second striking point in the creation of man is that God created man with a spirit.

The Breath of Life Breathed by God into Man's Body Formed with Dust

Genesis 2:7 says that God formed man of the dust of the ground. No doubt this refers to man's body as the framework of man's being. We do have a body formed with dust. Science tells us that our body is just a composition of the elements of the earth, just like dust. Whatever is in the dust is in our body. However, this is not all in God's creation of man. After God formed a body for man, God breathed the breath of life into man's nostrils. Dust does not have any life, but the breath of God has life. Therefore, God's breath is the breath of life.

In Genesis 2:7 the word for *breath* in Hebrew is *neshamah.* It is used also in Proverbs 20:27, which says, "The spirit of man is the candle [lamp] of the Lord." This indicates that the very breath of life breathed into man's body became man's spirit. This is confirmed by Job 32:8, which says, "But there is a spirit in man, and the breath of the Almighty gives them understanding." In this verse *a spirit in man* and *the breath of the Almighty* are in apposition, indicating that the spirit of man and the breath of God are one. The spirit of man is the breath of God, and the breath of God is man's spirit. God not only formed a body to be the frame of man, but He also produced a spirit to be the very inner organ within man. God has prepared a stomach in our physical body. The stomach is a physical organ for us to receive, digest, and assimilate food. In a similar way, God produced an inner organ, that is, our spirit, for us to use to contact God. This corresponds with the Lord's word in John 4:24: "God is Spirit, and those who worship Him must worship in spirit and truthfulness." Only spirit can contact Spirit. Only spirit can worship Spirit. God is Spirit, and we have a spirit so that we can worship God, we can contact God.

If we stay away from our spirit and remain in our mind, the more we think, the more we consider, the more we will feel that there is no God. But if we turn to our spirit in the inmost part of our being, we will spontaneously worship God, saying, "God, I thank You." To attempt to substantiate God by using our mind is like trying to smell a fragrance by using our eyes. Our eyes simply cannot smell the fragrance. Therefore, to us there is no fragrance, because we cannot see it. However, if we would cease trying to use our eyes and instead use our nose, we would surely smell the fragrance. God is a Spirit, and He prepared for us a spirit that we may worship Him, contact Him, receive Him, and even contain Him as our life and our everything. We Christians are no longer persons without God. Today we have God in our spirit. Therefore, we are not lifeless but are lively, full of life. We are organic. In this organic life God and we, we and God, have become one.

This Spirit of Man Being Ranked with the Heavens and the Earth in the Holy Word of God

We need to realize how important and crucial our spirit is. The spirit of man is ranked with the heavens and the earth in the holy Word of God. In Zechariah 12:1 the prophet Zechariah said that God stretches forth the heavens and lays the foundation of the earth and forms the spirit of man within him. According to this verse three things in the universe are crucial: the heavens, the earth, and our spirit. The heavens are for the earth; the earth is for man to exist; and the spirit of man is for God, to worship God (John 4:24), to be regenerated by God (John 3:6b), and to be joined to God (1 Cor. 6:17) that man may walk and live in the organic union with God (Gal. 5:16; Rom. 8:4b).

Our Need to Live and Walk by the Spirit

Although in the past we have received much teaching concerning our spirit, I am burdened about this matter again because I realize that out of one hundred saints, it is difficult to find one who lives in the spirit and walks according to the spirit. In Galatians 5:25 Paul said, "If we live by the Spirit, let us also walk by the Spirit," and in 5:16 he said, "But I say, Walk by the Spirit and you shall by no means fulfill the lust of the flesh." In Romans 8:4 Paul said that the believers should not walk according to the flesh but according to the spirit. According to these verses we all should walk by and according to the Spirit to the extent that we do everything according to the Spirit. Although this is clearly written in the Bible, we do not practice what the Bible says.

Through the years of my ministry I have contacted many different kinds of people. Out of one hundred I have not found one brother or sister who does everything according to the Spirit. In doing their shopping the sisters may shop mainly according to the sales advertised in the newspapers, not according to the Spirit. They may forget the heavens and the earth and not care for the Spirit within them. After they buy certain items, they may turn from their mind to their spirit and regret and even repent for what they have done. Nevertheless, the next week they may do the same thing again, forgetting the Spirit as they do their shopping.

The husbands all love their wife, but when they lose their temper toward their wife, they forget everything. Temper is aroused mainly by the exchanging of words. If the husband and the wife do not exchange words, there will be no temper. A little word from the wife to the husband may ignite the fire of temper within the husband. Our attempts to limit, restrict, and exercise self-control over our temper do not work. Therefore, the best way to avoid our temper is not to speak. The way to shut off our speaking is to do everything according to the Spirit. After a wife speaks an unpleasant word to her husband, the Spirit within him may tell him to be silent and not to do anything until the tempest has subsided and the Spirit gives him the liberty to act.

We all need to ask ourselves whether we live a life that is according to the Spirit or not. Because I do not live fully according to the Spirit, again and again I must confess to the Lord and ask Him to forgive me for doing something not according to my spirit. We are not used to living according to the Spirit. Instead, we are very accustomed to living according to our mind, our emotion, or our will. In the meetings of the church we may behave somewhat according to the Spirit, but after the meeting is dismissed, we may forget the Spirit again and not live according to Him. This is the real situation in the church life.

The spirit prepared by God for us is the highest part of our being. The highest part of our being is not the flesh, not the body, but the spirit. Whatever we do according to our body is low and even mean. If we do everything according to our spirit, we are honorable and are living on the highest level. When a wife says something to her husband, the husband should not answer quickly but should answer according to his spirit. He should respond according to the Spirit. Likewise, in dealing with their children, the parents should do it according to the Spirit. In Ephesians 6:4 Paul said, "And fathers, do not provoke your children to anger." The only way for parents to rebuke their children without provoking them is to do it in their spirit. When parents are going to rebuke their children, they should prepare themselves to do it according to the Spirit. Then, their rebuking will be a pleasant thing to the children. Otherwise, if the rebuking is administered out of the parents' flesh, it will provoke the children. The Bible tells us that parents should chastise and discipline their children (Prov. 19:18; 22:15; 23:13-14; 29:15). The unique way for the parents to do this without provoking their children is to do it according to the Spirit.

Romans 8:4 speaks of the righteous requirement of the law being fulfilled in those who walk according to the spirit, that is, the regenerated human spirit indwelt and mingled with the Spirit, who is the consummation of the Triune God. This verse indicates that we can be justified by God in His presence only if we do everything according to the spirit. If we do not conduct ourselves according to the spirit, we cannot be justified before God. Many believers who hold the so-called reformed theology do not care for the subjective experiences of Christ; they care only for the objective side of Christian experience. They say that since Christ is our righteousness, we are justified by God. Although this is true, it is only a part of the proper theology. The Bible tells us that justification is first objective (Rom. 3:24, 26) and then subjective (Rom. 4:25 and note 1; Rev. 19:8 and note 2). First, Christ is our righteousness objectively for us to be justified by God that we may be saved. However, if we are going on to live as a child of God and a member of Christ, we must live Christ (Gal. 2:20; Phil. 1:19-21), making Christ also our subjective righteousness (Phil. 3:9). In Galatians 2:20 the apostle Paul said, "I am crucified with Christ; and it is no longer I who live, but it is Christ who lives in me." Then, in Philippians 2:12-13 Paul told the believers to work out their own salvation, for it is God who operates in them both the willing and the working for His good pleasure. God not only lives in us, but He even operates in us.

In His creation of man God produced a spirit for man. According to Genesis 2:7, the issue of God's breathing the breath of life into man's body of dust was that man became a living soul. Thus, man is a tripartite being of body, soul, and spirit. Man's body is his outer frame, his spirit is his inmost organ, and his soul is his inner being, his person. In the New Testament Paul said, "And the God of peace Himself sanctify you wholly, and may your spirit and soul and body be preserved complete, without blame, at the coming of our Lord Jesus Christ" (1 Thes. 5:23), confirming that man is tripartite.

Although the details of God's creation of man may be familiar to us, we need to be reminded that day by day we should live Christ, doing everything according to the inner spirit. In 2 Timothy 4:22 Paul said, "The Lord be with your spirit." Christ is with our spirit. This is all that we need. We need Christ within our spirit that we may live Him. We should not live a Chinese, an American, a German, or a Frenchman; we should live Christ by doing everything according to our spirit. In doing everything we should not do it by our self but by Christ according to our spirit. Then we will live Christ.

We have not been fully faithful to what we have heard of the Lord through the years. In this one thing we have all offended the Lord—in our not living Him by doing everything according to the Spirit. In God's creation of man, God purposely breathed the breath of life into man that man might have an inmost organ to contact God, to make man himself a God-man. This is to be a human being by exercising our spirit in everything. We need to practice this; otherwise, we can never be a proper Christian. We may speak, teach, preach, and expound the Bible to others, but if we do not do everything according to the Spirit, we are practicing hypocrisy and falsehood. We may claim that we are loving the Lord and seeking Him, and that we are in His recovery for His testimony, yet we may be persons who do things not according to the Spirit. Instead, we may do things according to right and wrong, by avoiding what is wrong and doing our best to do what is right. However, it is possible to do many right things without doing them according to the Spirit. To do things according to right and wrong is based on the principle of the tree of the knowledge of good and evil; to do everything according to the Spirit is based on the principle of the tree of life.

PUTTING MAN BEFORE THE TREE OF LIFE

The third striking point in God's creation of man is that after God created man, He put man before the tree of life (Gen. 2:8-9). The man created by God was complete and perfect, having a body and a spirit with a soul. God put this complete and perfect man in front of the tree of life.

The figure of the tree of life in the Bible has puzzled nearly all the Bible teachers. In the Bible the tree of life is mentioned first in Genesis 2, and it proceeds through the Bible to the end, to Revelation 22. Between the two ends of the Bible, in Revelation 2:7 the Lord promised the overcomers that He will give them to eat of the tree of life. In order to discover what the tree of life is, we need to read through the Bible, beginning from Genesis 2. Eventually, we will reach Psalm 36:9, which says, "For with You is the fountain of life." According to this verse, with God is the fountain of life. The tree of life must be something that is related to life. Where is life? Life is in God. With God there is the fountain of life. Thus, God is the fountain, the source, of life. After reading further, we come to the New Testament. In John 1:4 we read, "In Him was life." The word *Him* in this verse refers to the Word in verse 1, who is God Himself. In the Word, who is God, is life. In John 14:6 this One came and told us, "I am ...the life," and in John 15:1 He said, "I am the true vine." Besides Christ, every vine is a false one. Only He is the true vine. A vine is a tree. If we put these two matters, life and the tree, together, we have the tree of life. Who is the tree of life? The tree of life is the Triune God, who embodied Himself in Christ. Christ as the embodiment of the Triune God is the life in the vine tree. Therefore, Christ is the tree of life.

The tree of life is a vine tree, not a pine tree. A pine grows by shooting upward, into the heavens, but a vine grows by stretching forth to reach people. Since Christ is a vine, everyone can partake of His fruit. If He were a pine, it would be difficult for us to touch Him. Ultimately, the tree of life is described in Revelation 22:2: "And on this side and on that side of the river was the tree of life, producing twelve fruits, yielding its fruit each month; and the leaves of the tree are for the healing of the nations." From this verse we can see that the tree of life does not grow by shooting upward; rather, it grows along the river of water of life, on the two sides of the river. A tree that grows along the two sides of a river surely must be a vine.

A vine tree is not for producing material for the construction of a building; a vine tree is good only for producing fruit. The fruit of the vine is for two purposes. First, the fruit is for the propagation and multiplication of the vine. Second, it is for food to provide nourishment to the eaters. Christ today is just such a vine, bearing fruit for His propagation and multiplication and for our nourishment.

In brief, the tree of life in the Bible is a figure of the Triune God embodied in Christ to be the very substance of the divine life. This tree is good for man to take and eat (Gen. 2:16; John 6:57b) that man may be constituted with God as the constituent of life. Thus, man and God become organically united and live together as one person (John 15:5; Phil. 1:20-21a). Colossians 3:4 says that Christ is our life.

Therefore, we need to take Him as our supply, as the very substance of the divine life, in which life we can be victorious and overcoming and can be so high that we can even reign in His eternal life (Rom. 5:17). We can be kings in the eternal life. Eventually, we will be co-kings with Christ in the thousand-year kingdom (Rev. 3:21; 20:4).

However, according to my observation, I have not been able to find one dear saint through the years who truly lives not himself but Christ. We all have two lives. We have the natural life, the human life, and we have the spiritual life, the divine life. The natural life is just us, ourselves; and the divine life is also a person, Christ. Each one of us is two persons, one person being our self and the other being Christ in us. As two persons, we have two lives, our natural life and the divine life. We have the life from Adam and we have the life that is Christ Himself in us.

The problem is, by what life will we live? By the first life or the second life? By the natural life or the divine life? By our self or by Christ? I say again that I have not found anyone, even one who is very much in the church life, who lives Christ day by day and hour after hour and does not live himself. Hymns #841, 499, and 501 *(Hymns)* speak of living Christ and not ourselves. We need to check to see if our life matches the standard expressed in these hymns. We need to realize that we were created to be like God, even to be one with God. Furthermore, we have been saved into God to be regenerated by Him that we may be His children and may be members of Christ to constitute the Body of Christ. However, we need to ask ourselves whether we live God or not. We do have a marvelous provision. God has provided us with a body and with a spirit, which are very sufficient for us to live as a man to worship God, to receive God, and to contain God that we may live God and express Him.

Even after being saved by God, we may not live Him. We may be gentlemen, men who are right, but we may not be able to say, "It is no longer I who live, but it is Christ who lives in me" (Gal 2:20a). We may not be able to apply this holy word to ourselves. We need to realize the organic union between us and God. We need to behave ourselves, to walk, to live, to do everything, in this organic union. It should not be I but Christ; it should not be I by myself, but I with God, united, mingled, and blended to be one person, a God-man.

Chapter Two

IN INCARNATION

Scripture Reading: Eph. 1:5, 9-11; 3:9; Gen. 3:15; Isa. 7:14; Gal. 4:4; Matt. 1:20, 16; Gen. 22:18; Gal. 3:16; Matt. 1:1; John 1:1, 14, 16-17; Rom. 8:3m; John 1:1-4a; 14:6a; 10:10b; 12:24; 1 Cor. 15:45b; 2 Cor. 3:17-18; John 20:22; Col. 3:4a; 1 Cor. 6:17; John 15:1, 5; Gal. 2:20a; Phil. 1:20-21a

OUTLINE

I. God's eternal good pleasure of His will:
  - A. As unveiled to the apostle Paul—Eph. 1:5, 9, 11.
  - B. To be one with man.
  - C. Becoming His eternal economy—Eph. 1:10; 3:9.

II. God's promise to come to be the seed of man:
  - A. To be the seed of woman—Gen. 3:15; Isa. 7:14; Gal. 4:4; Matt. 1:20, 16.
  - B. To be the seed of Abraham—Gen. 22:18; Gal. 3:16; Matt. 1:1.

III. The fulfillment of God's good pleasure and promise:
  - A. The Word as the defined and explained God becoming flesh—John 1:1, 14a; Rom. 8:3m.
  - B. To be a Man, to be one with man that man may be one with God.
  - C. Tabernacling among men, full of God's grace and reality—John 1:14, 16-17.

IV. To bring God as life to man:
  - A. The life of God being in the incarnated Word—John 1:1-4a; 14:6a.
  - B. Coming to bring God's life to man abundantly—John 10:10b.
  - C. Dying to release the divine life—John 12:24.

- D. Becoming the life-giving Spirit in resurrection—1 Cor. 15:45b; 2 Cor. 3:17-18.
- E. Entering into His believers to be their life—John 20:22; Col. 3:4a.

V. That He may be one with the believing people:

- A. To be one spirit—1 Cor. 6:17.
- B. In the organic union of the divine life.
- C. Making God and man one person, signified by the true vine—John 15:1:
  1. The two coinhering—John 15:5.
  2. The first living in the second—Gal. 2:20a.
  3. The second living in the first to manifest Him—Phil. 1:20-21a.

THE CREATION OF MAN IN GOD'S IMAGE AND ACCORDING TO GOD'S LIKENESS

God's Image and Likeness Being Organic

We have seen that God created man in a particular way. First, He created man in His image and according to His likeness (Gen. 1:26). This means that God created man in a living way, because His image and likeness are not lifeless, outward forms but are organic and full of life. Both God's image and God's likeness are organic. The image of God is what He is. What He is as the living God is living and organic. Likewise, since God's likeness is the expression of what He is, His likeness also must be organic. Therefore, the man created by God is a living entity, because this man was created in God's image and according to God's likeness, both of which are living and organic.

Man's Body Being from the Dust and Man's Spirit Being from the Breath of Life

Second, God made a spirit for man (Gen. 2:7). To make man in God's image and likeness did not require any material, but to make a body, a frame, for man required some material. The material used by God to make man's body is dust (Gen. 2:7a). Anything made of dust is lifeless because there is no life in dust. Thus, in itself man's body, man's frame, is lifeless. After forming man's body from dust, God then made another part for man—the inmost part. This part is called the spirit (v. 7b).

God made a spirit in man with His own breath. God's breath of life is the material with which God made a spirit within man. Proverbs 20:27 says, "The spirit of man is the candle [lamp] of the Lord." The word *spirit* in this verse is *neshamah* in Hebrew, the same word for *breath* in Genesis 2:7. Thus, the breath of life in Genesis 2:7 is the spirit of man in Proverbs 20:27. This is confirmed by Job 32:8, which says, "But there is a spirit in man, and the breath of the Almighty gives them understanding." *The breath of the Almighty* in the second clause is in apposition to *a spirit in man* in the first clause. Therefore, the breath of the Almighty is the spirit in man.

Something in man's makeup is very close to God and is related to God. It is not God the Spirit nor God's life, but God's breath of life—something very close to life. It is not life, but it is the breath of life. God breathed this part of Himself into man's body. The breath of God, after being breathed into man's body, became man's spirit. With this part man can contact God.

Man's Spirit Being the Organ to Contact God

In order to substantiate anything, we must use the proper organ. In our body we have many organs, including two ears for hearing, two eyes for seeing, a nose for smelling, and a tongue for tasting. In order to see colors, we must use the right organ. It is impossible to smell colors; but we can see colors. In order to contact God, we must use the proper organ—our spirit. God is Spirit (John 4:24). God cannot be realized by the mind. God is a spiritual entity, a spiritual reality. In order to realize Him we need to use the proper organ. Some people who are atheists say strongly that there is no God. During the day they may give lectures to people, stating strongly that there is no God. But at night when they go back home, something within checks with them, "Suppose there is a God. What would you do?" If we would turn from our thinking mind to our innermost part, our spirit, spontaneously we would say, "O God!" and God's presence would be realized by us. Our spirit is an organ particularly made by God with His own breath of life. We do have such an organ that is crucially related to God. Because of this, in John 4:24 the Lord Jesus told us, "God is Spirit, and those who worship Him must worship in spirit [man's spirit]."

Man Being according to God's Kind

Man was created by God as an entity with a frame, the outer part, and a spirit, the inmost organ. Hence, man was created as a complete person. But what is God's purpose in making such a man? God created the heavens, the earth, and myriads of living things: the herbs, the trees, the fish in the water, the birds in the air, and the beasts, the cattle, and all kinds of creeping things on the earth (Gen. 1:11-25). In addition to all these things, God made man in a very particular way—like God. Man was not made according to the "kind" of the herbs or the kind of the trees. Neither was man made according to the kind of the animals, the beasts, or the cattle. Man was made according to God's kind.

Man cannot be God in His Godhead, but he can be God in His life and nature. We are what we are born of. Anything born of a dog is a dog. Likewise, if we were born of a monkey, we would surely be a monkey. God created man not according to a monkey's kind or a dog's kind, but according to His kind, in His image and according to His likeness. Furthermore, the Bible tells us that the believers in Christ are God's children (John 1:12-13; 1 John 3:1-2). The children of a man are also men. Because we are children of God, we are God in nature and in life, but not in the Godhead, that is, not in God's position or rank.

Man Needing to Eat the Tree of Life

Although the man created by God was complete, having God's image and likeness and God's breath of life, man was still short of God Himself. Apparently, the created man was perfect; actually, he was not perfect because, although he was like God, he did not have God Himself. Thus, after the creation of man, God did not tell man what to do. He did not regulate man or give him many commandments. He simply brought man into a garden and put him in front of a strange, peculiar, and particular tree called the tree of life (Gen. 2:8-9). Since the tree of knowledge of good and evil was next to the tree of life, God warned man not to eat of it, lest he die (vv. 16-17). If he ate of that tree, he would receive death. On the other hand, if he ate of the tree of life, he would receive life. God's warning to Adam indicates that God wanted man to take of the tree of life.

The Tree of Life Signifying God as Life to Man

The Bible is God's revelation, consisting of sixty-six books with hundreds of chapters. The Bible ends as it begins. It has a beginning and it also has an ending. The end is exactly the same as the beginning. The Bible begins with God, man, and the tree of life in Genesis 1 and 2, and it ends with God, man, and the tree of life in Revelation 22.

The tree of life is revealed gradually throughout the entire Bible. Psalm 36:9 says, "For with You [God] is the fountain of life." God Himself is the fountain of life. The first chapter of the Gospel of John says, "In the beginning was the Word... and the Word was God.... In Him was life" (vv. 1, 4). Later in this same Gospel, the Lord Jesus told us that He is the life and that He is the true vine (14:6; 15:1). He is not a pine tree, shooting upward, but a vine tree, spreading forward to reach men. Eventually, at the end of the New Testament, the tree of life as a vine tree is there (Rev. 22:2). In the New Jerusalem the river of water of life flows through the city to water the entire city in every part, and the tree of life grows along the two sides of the river. Such a tree could not be a tall tree like a pine; it must be a vine. Because it is a vine, its fruit is accessible to everyone. This is very meaningful.

The tree of life at the beginning and end of the Bible is a figure of God Himself as life. God is abstract and mysterious. There is no word that can fully define Him. Hence, in His wisdom He presented us a figure of Himself—a tree that grows, spreads, and produces fruit good for food. The tree of life is a figure signifying God as life to man. This tree of life is the embodiment of God as life. God presented Himself to man in this way. After He created man, God had no intention to charge man to do anything. His intention was just to work Himself into man.

God created man with a body as an outward frame and with a spirit inside this body. But how could God enter into man? The way for God to enter into man was to bring man into a garden and put him before the tree of life. The tree of life is God Himself embodied in the form of a tree. In form and style, it is a tree, but actually it is the very embodiment of the divine life. Eventually, this embodiment is Jesus Christ. When the Son of God came to this earth, He came as the embodiment of the Triune God (Col. 2:9; 1:19). The Triune God is life, and this life is embodied in the tree of life, which is a figure of Christ. Thus, when Christ came, He told us that He is life (John 14:6) and that He is the vine tree (15:1), of which we can be a part (v. 5). If we put these two things together—life and the tree—we have the tree of life. Christ Himself is the tree of life.

After He completed His creation of man, God offered Himself to man in the form of a tree. Eating is the way for man to take this tree. This tree is not good for material or for making anything. This tree is good only for producing fruit for man to eat. As the tree of life, God cherishes and nourishes man. This tree of life is the Christ in whom we have believed. God presented this tree to all mankind through the preaching of the gospel, and we accepted it. Daily we are eating Him (John 6:57) as our tree of life. Our vine tree is Christ, and Christ is the embodiment of God as life (1 John 5:11-12). Thus, the Bible says that Christ is our life (Col. 3:4a). We live by Him, we live for Him, we express Him, and we magnify Him. This is what a Christian should be.

GOD'S ETERNAL GOOD PLEASURE OF HIS WILL

Before God created anything, He had a good pleasure within Him (Eph. 1:5, 9). This pleasure became His will, which eventually became His purpose. This purpose then became His economy through His counsel (vv. 9-11; 3:9). Through a council held among the three of the Trinity (Gen. 1:26), God made a counsel to create man and even to become a man. Hence, God created man according to His good pleasure. After creating everything, He looked on what He had made, including man, and said that it was very good (Gen. 1:31). God created man with a body and with a spirit and placed him before the tree of life. This was the first step. But man still did not have God. Thus, God had to take a further step, the step of becoming a man.

GOD'S PROMISE TO COME TO BE THE SEED OF MAN

Do not think that it was easy for God to enter into man. He first created man, and then He waited. God is a God who is patience; therefore, He can be patient. After creating man, He waited four thousand years before He came to be a man.

The first promise that He would come was given to Adam (Gen. 3:15), and the second promise, two thousand years later, was given to Abraham (22:18). Still, He did not come; rather, He waited another two thousand years. Then one day, two thousand years ago, He came, not in the way of coming down from the third heaven and appearing suddenly as a man on the earth, but by entering into the womb of a human virgin. He was born there and remained in that womb for nine months (Matt. 1:20). Then He was delivered out of the womb of that virgin, and He became a child in the manger at Bethlehem (Luke 2:16). This child was called the Mighty God and the Eternal Father (Isa. 9:6). He was also called Emmanuel—God with us (Matt. 1:23). He is God with man, and He is a man.

To Be the Seed of Woman

After the first step of God's creation of man, man became fallen (Gen. 3:1-6). Then God came in, not to condemn man or to curse man, but to give man a promise that the seed of the woman would come to bruise the head of the damaging serpent (v. 15; Isa. 7:14; Gal. 4:4; Matt. 1:20, 16). That promise indicated that God Himself would come to be the seed of woman.

To Be the Seed of Abraham

After the promise given to Adam, God waited two thousand years until the time of Abraham. He then made a further promise to Abraham, saying, "And in thy seed shall all the nations of the earth be blessed" (Gen. 22:18; Gal. 3:16; Matt. 1:1). According to Galatians 3:14, the promise given to Abraham was that God Himself would come to be the seed of Abraham, and this seed would be a blessing to all the nations by becoming the all-inclusive Spirit for mankind to receive.

THE FULFILLMENT OF GOD'S GOOD PLEASURE AND PROMISE

The Word as the Defined and Explained God Becoming Flesh

After His promise to Abraham, God waited another two

thousand years before coming to be a man named Jesus Christ, who was also called Emmanuel—God with us. Through His incarnation He as the Word, the defined and explained God, became flesh (John 1:1, 14a; Rom. 8:3m).

Since that time two thousand years have passed. A total of six thousand years have passed since the creation of Adam: two thousand years from Adam to Abraham, two thousand years from Abraham until the day God became incarnated to be a man, and two thousand years from that day until today.

To Be a Man, to Be One with Man That Man May Be One with God

God created man with the desire that one day He would enter into man. The created man had His image, His likeness, and His breath of life as man's spirit, but he did not have God. God created man for the purpose that He would enter into man to be one with man, to make man one with Him. This is the organic union. Today we have God in us. Therefore, we have an organic union with God.

Tabernacling among Men, Full of God's Grace and Reality

After four thousand years God Himself became a man through a part of man, a virgin. Through this human virgin He picked up the likeness of man's flesh (Rom. 8:3). As God who became a man, He has divinity, and He also has humanity. He is one person with divinity and humanity. He is both divine and human; He is both God and man. He is the complete God plus the perfect man. He is the God-man. As the God-man He tabernacled among men, full of God's grace and reality (John 1:14, 16-17).

TO BRING GOD AS LIFE TO MAN

The incarnation was to bring God as life to man. The life of God is in the incarnated Word (John 1:1-4a; 14:6a), and this incarnated Word came to bring God's life to man abundantly (10:10b). Eventually, He died as a grain of wheat to release the divine life (12:24), and He became the life-giving Spirit in His resurrection (1 Cor. 15:45b; 2 Cor. 3:17-18). As such a life-giving Spirit He enters into His believers to be their life (John 20:22; Col. 3:4a).

The God-man Jesus is the fulfillment of God's good pleasure and promise. However, this God-man was alone, by Himself. God's desire is that this God-man would enter into us to be our life. God created man, including us, and He became a man. But now He wants to enter into our being. After being born to be a God-man, He lived on earth for thirty-three and a half years, traveling back and forth, from Bethlehem to Nazareth and from Nazareth to Jerusalem. Then He was put on the cross to be killed, to be terminated. Afterward, He was resurrected, and in resurrection He as a God-man and the last Adam became a life-giving Spirit. At the same time, in His resurrection, He resurrected us and regenerated us (Eph. 2:6; 1 Pet. 1:3). In His resurrection He included us. When we were resurrected with Him, we all were regenerated. We were resurrected before we were born. This is God's economy. At the time of our resurrection with Christ, we all received His divine and resurrected life into us. In resurrection He was born to be the firstborn Son of God (Acts 13:33), and we were born with Him to be the many sons of God (Rom. 8:29). It was in this way that He entered into His believers.

After entering into His believers to be their life, He ascended (Acts 1:9). From the heavens He poured Himself out as the consummated, compounded, all-inclusive Spirit upon His disciples (2:1-4). Through this the church was established and began to carry out His commission to disciple all the nations (Matt. 28:19).

Eventually, the church reached even China, where I was saved. At first when I heard the gospel I did not like it, and I would not believe. I did not like this "foreign religion." But gradually, I believed, even against my wishes and against my will. After I believed, I began to be bothered, because something entered into me. This I cannot deny. This made me happy and even made me a different person. Today I am not merely a man; I am a God-filled man. I am a man who has God in him. Today I am living God, expressing God, and magnifying God. God is my life, and I am His expression.

THAT HE MAY BE ONE WITH THE BELIEVING PEOPLE

After entering into His believing people, God becomes one spirit with them (1 Cor. 6:17) in the organic union of the divine life. In this organic union God and man are one person, signified by the true vine in John 15:1. In the organic union the vine and the branches coinhere; the vine abides in the branches and the branches abide in the vine (v. 5). The first, the vine, lives in the second, the branches (Gal. 2:20a), and the second lives in the first to manifest Him (Phil. 1:20-21a).

THE ORGANIC UNION IN INCARNATION

We may think that the incarnation lasted for only nine months. However, the incarnation of God for Him to enter into man has been going on for two thousand years, from the first century to the twentieth century. One afternoon in April 1925, at the age of nineteen, I heard the wonderful gospel. As a result, I opened myself and received God into me. I became a different person. At that juncture God was incarnated into me. Although at times I even tried to deny that God was in me, I cannot deny that from the hour of my conversion God has been in me.

God is still going to be incarnated into many thousands of people. How fast could this take place? It depends on us. If we would go and disciple the nations quickly, God would be incarnated in a fast way. God's incarnation is just to carry out God's desire with His good pleasure to be one with man in the organic union. Through God's incarnation man is in an organic union with the organic God.

God created man, and then He came to be a man in incarnation. After passing through the processes of human living, crucifixion, resurrection, ascension, and descension, He as the life-giving Spirit, who is the consummated, compound Spirit, entered into us. This is the completion of His incarnation. Now we are here in a completed union with God organically.

This is God's creation, this is God's incarnation, and this is our conversion. He created us six thousand years ago, He became us two thousand years ago, and He entered into us to be us today. Thus, we are a part of Him. We are His counterpart. A counterpart of God is just a part of God. What He is, we are. He is the Head and we are the Body. We cannot say that the Head is God and that the Body is not God. The Body and the Head are one and the same.

To be a Christian is not only to be moral with a high standard of morality. To be a Christian is to be God, to be a part of God, to be a counterpart of God. As Christians, we should live God, express God, and manifest God by walking and doing everything in the Spirit and according to the Spirit. The very God whose counterpart we have become is the life-giving, compound, all-inclusive Spirit, who is the consummation, the totality, the aggregate, of the processed Triune God. Such a Spirit is the great blessing to all the nations on this earth in Jesus Christ.

Chapter Three

IN SALVATION

Scripture Reading: Rom. 5:18b, 21b; 1 John 5:11-12; Rom. 5:10; Acts 11:18; Gen. 3:24; Heb. 10:19-20; Rev. 2:7; Heb. 4:16; Eph. 2:18; 1 Pet. 1:3; John 1:12-13; Col. 3:4a; 2 Pet. 1:4b; 1 John 4:13; Phil. 2:15-16; Matt. 5:16

OUTLINE

I. Through the all-inclusive redemption:
  A. Redeeming God's chosen people as sinners to be justified by God unto life, even unto the reign in the eternal life—the Triune God—Rom. 5:18b, 21b; 1 John 5:11-12.
  B. Reconciling the redeemed and justified sinners as God's enemies that they may be saved in the divine life of Christ—Rom. 5:10.
  C. Repentance unto life—Acts 11:18.

II. Unto the dynamic salvation of God:
  A. Cutting the way which had been closed to the fallen sinners to prevent them from eating the tree of life—Gen. 3:24; Heb. 10:19-20.
  B. Bringing the fallen sinners back to the tree of life, to God as life—Rev. 2:7; Heb. 4:16; Eph. 2:18.
  C. That the redeemed sinners may have an organic union with the redeeming God in order to be one with Him.
  D. To be regenerated by God and become His children—1 Pet. 1:3; John 1:12-13:
    1. Having God's life and nature—Col. 3:4a; 2 Pet. 1:4b.
    2. Possessing even the entire person of God—1 John 4:13.

3. That God may abide in the redeemed sinners and they in God.
4. For them to live God, manifesting and expressing Him—Phil. 2:15-16; Matt. 5:16.
5. Thus, the redeemed sinners may become God in life and nature in their organic union with God by the Spirit of God—1 John 4:13.

A HEAVENLY AND DIVINE VIEW

We need a clear, heavenly, and divine view. Thank the Lord that the Bible, the holy Word, does give us such a view. However, in order to see such a view, we need to jump out of the limitation of the letter of the Bible. In 2 Corinthians 3:6 Paul said, "The letter kills, but the Spirit gives life." We need to jump out of the letter and jump into the Spirit by prayer. By our looking to the Lord continually, the vision comes, and this vision brings in a view.

God's Purpose to Work Himself into Man

In this view God is infinite and unlimited, having no beginning and no ending. This marvelously great God is a God of purpose. The greater a person is, the greater the purpose he has. Because we are living, we all have a purpose. God also has a purpose (Eph. 3:10-11), and this purpose is just to obtain what He desires to have. His heart's desire is His good pleasure (1:9). This good pleasure is revealed in Paul's writings, especially in the book of Ephesians. God's good pleasure forms the will of God, and for this will God held a council in His Divine Trinity to make a counsel (v. 11b). There is such a counsel in the whole universe. This counsel is that God intends to work Himself into man. This is a great matter. For the almighty, unlimited, infinite God to work Himself into the small, limited, finite man to be one with this man is a great thing.

God's Creation according to His Purpose

According to His counsel, His will, His good pleasure, and His heart's desire, in time God came to create (Rev. 4:11). First, He created the heavens with all the angels (Gen. 1:1; Job 38:7). At that time none of the angels understood what God was doing. Then God created the earth, a small "ball" in the universe. On this earth God created many different kinds of life in three levels: the vegetable life to show the beauty of the earth (Gen. 1:11-12), the animal life to show the livingness of the earth (vv. 24-25), and the human life to indicate the purpose of God on the earth (vv. 26-28). The vegetable life is the lowest form of life, and the animal life is a higher form of life. The human life is higher still, but it is not the highest life. In Genesis 1 we can see the three levels of life on the earth. Then, in Genesis 2 God brought the completed man as the high life on this earth to a tree—not an apple tree but a tree of life, a life tree (vv. 8-9). This tree of life is the embodiment of life. The life embodied in the tree of life is not the vegetable life nor the animal life nor the human life, but the divine life.

God intended that His created man with the human life would take Him as the highest life that he might be no longer merely a man but a God-man, no longer merely human, but divinely human. It is possible that we have been reading the Bible for many years and yet have never seen such a view. This view is the central thought of the holy Word.

God's Promise of His Salvation to Man

In Genesis 3 the man created by God was seduced by Satan through the serpent and became fallen (vv. 1-6). At such a juncture it seemed that everything was finished; but God is never finished. He would never give up. He came in to seek and to find this fallen man. God said to Adam, "Where are you?" Adam was frightened, trembling, and naked, and he hid himself from God (vv. 9-10). Then God comforted Adam, indicating that he did not need to be afraid of the serpent, for God Himself would be incarnated as the seed of woman to crush the head of the evil one (v. 15). After hearing God's word of comfort, Adam was happy. That word was God's first promise to man, indicating that the very God who created man would one day come to be a man. God seemed to say to Adam, "Wait, Adam; I will become a man. In other words, I will become you. I am the almighty, infinite, unlimited, eternal God, but one day I will be just like you. Now you are in the flesh, and I will be in the likeness of your flesh." Although Adam was happy because of God's promise, he did not see the fulfillment of that promise.

After giving His word of promise to Adam, God was patient and waited for two thousand years, apparently doing nothing to fulfill His word. Then God came in to make another promise, this time to Abraham: "And in thy seed shall all the nations of the earth be blessed" (22:18). God's promise to Abraham was that one of his seed, one of his descendants, would come to be the factor through which the entire earth would be blessed. According to Galatians 3:14 and 16, this blessing was that through faith in Christ, the unique seed of Abraham, all the nations would receive the Triune God as the all-inclusive, life-giving Spirit. No doubt Abraham was happy about this promise, but he did not see its fulfillment.

The Eternal God Incarnated to Be a Man

After another two thousand years—altogether approximately four thousand years after the creation of Adam—Israel was under the tyranny of the Roman Empire. Nevertheless, there was still a small inn in Bethlehem to which God could come to be born into humanity. Eventually, God came through a virgin and lay in a manger as a small child. That child was the mighty God and the eternal Father (Isa. 9:6). He was the One promised initially as the seed of woman and again as the seed of Abraham to bless all the world with Himself as the consummated Spirit. Although we have a clear view today, at that time no one knew the significance of what was taking place. Herod hated Him and wanted to kill Him. In his attempt to do away with Christ, Herod slew many children (Matt. 2:7-8, 16-18). But this One escaped to Egypt, and after Herod's death He returned to the land of Israel (vv. 13-15).

In the Sunday schools many children are taught the story of Jesus' birth in Bethlehem and His lying in a manger, but who understands the intrinsic significance of such a story? That is not merely a story; that is the account of the infinite God becoming a man! This is a great thing, for that child lying in a manger was the almighty God, the infinite, eternal One, who became a man.

Dying an All-inclusive Death and Entering into an All-producing Resurrection

As a man He needed to grow. Thirty years were assigned to Him for His growth. When He became thirty years of age, He came out to minister for God's economy. Eventually, people, under the instigation of Satan, put Him on the cross and crucified Him. This fulfilled God's economy. Through His crucifixion on the cross, He died an all-inclusive death—not a common death that is hated by man but an all-inclusive death that is loved by His believers. There is a cross in the universe that has accomplished an all-inclusive death. This death terminated Satan (Heb. 2:14), the world (John 12:31), the old creation (Col. 1:15b), the fallen man (Rom. 6:6), man's sinful constitution (8:3), and everything negative in the universe. This all-inclusive death was not only a terminating death but also a releasing death, for through it the divine life was released from the human shell of the man Jesus Christ (John 12:24).

After accomplishing such an all-inclusive death, Christ entered into rest and was buried. Then, after three days He resurrected. His death was all-inclusive—terminating, redeeming, and releasing—and His resurrection was all-producing. In His resurrection a life-giving Spirit was produced (1 Cor. 15:45). Before Christ's resurrection, there was not such a life-giving Spirit in the universe. John 7:39 says that "the Spirit was not yet, because Jesus had not yet been glorified"; that is, Jesus had not yet entered into resurrection (Luke 24:26). On the day that He entered into resurrection, the life-giving Spirit was produced. His resurrection also produced Him as the firstborn Son of God (Acts 13:33). In eternity He was the only begotten Son of God (John 1:18), but in resurrection He was born to be the firstborn Son of God. With Him, thousands of sons of God were born (1 Pet. 1:3). How producing the resurrection of Christ was!

Today in the universe there are three particular categories of things: 1) the life-giving Spirit, 2) the firstborn Son of God, and 3) the many sons of God. Today we are the many sons of God. These many sons are the counterpart of God. As the many sons of God, we are a part of God. He is the Head and we are the Body (Col. 1:18a; Eph. 5:30). Therefore, we are a part of God. Within us He is the life-giving Spirit, and this life-giving Spirit is the pneumatic Christ (2 Cor. 3:17), who is the embodiment of the Triune God (Col. 2:9).

Ascending to Be Made the Lord, the Christ, the Leader, and the Savior

After He died and resurrected, He ascended to the heavens to be officially appointed, established, and made the Lord of all, the Christ of God, the Leader of all the kings on this earth, and the Savior (Acts 2:36; 5:31; Rev. 1:5). As such a One, He has the full right and the authority to manage the entire world so that He can save people. If He were not such a Leader, we would not have been and could not have been saved. We have been saved because He is not only the Savior but also the Ruler of the whole earth.

Although I was born in faraway China, the ascended Christ sent missionaries to China by means of imperialism. Even imperialism was used by Christ to save me and many others in China. God is Christ, and Christ now is the Lord of all, the Christ of God, the Leader of all the rulers on this earth, and the Savior.

Saving Us by Entering into Us to Consummate the Divine Incarnation

Such a One is now ready to save us by entering into us. We had fallen into death and even into hell and the lake of fire. He did not save us by reaching down and snatching us up. He saved us by entering into us as the all-inclusive Spirit, as the consummation of the Triune God. As a result, we became so buoyant that we rose up to become a part of God. This is Christ's salvation.

Today He is not only in us, but He is everywhere. He fills all in all (Eph. 1:23b). He is not only all-inclusive; He is also all-extensive. Although He fills all in all, He takes us particularly as His dwelling. Now He is even making His home in our hearts (3:17). By doing so, He is building a home for Himself. He is everywhere, but particularly He is in us, taking us as His principal dwelling, making us His home. If we see this, we will be buoyant and will soar in the air. We have no other place to go but to Him. He is our Savior; He is our Redeemer; He is our life; He is our everything; and He is our eternal home. Today we are remaining in Him, abiding in Him, and living in Him to have our life in Him. This is why we are full of joy.

Up to this point the very Triune God still has not completed His incarnation. Since His passing through crucifixion, resurrection, and ascension, and after His pouring out of Himself, His incarnation has proceeded for another two thousand years. In these past twenty centuries He has been transfusing and also infusing Himself into millions of His believers, including you and me. He has transfused Himself into us, and He is now infusing us every day. Because of His transfusing and infusing, the more I speak, the more I have to speak. I cannot finish my speaking. Under His transfusing and infusing, we are all here becoming the very consummation of the divine incarnation.

THE INTRINSIC VIEW OF GOD'S SALVATION

Now we need to consider what God's salvation is. Many Christians have been taught that we were sinners, and our destiny was to go to hell. Because God loved us, He sent His Son to die for our sins and to be resurrected to be our Savior. If we believe in Him, our sins will be forgiven. Then we will be saved by God and will have peace and joy. After being saved, we need to behave ourselves. Eventually, we will go to heaven. To many Christians, this is God's salvation. Although such a view may be biblical, it is according to the Bible in a superficial way. To understand the Bible in this way is like skating on ice. In studying the Bible, we need to cut a hole in the ice and dive to the bottom of the ocean to see what is there. It is there that we will see the depths, the very intrinsic significance, of the holy Word.

The salvation of God is not a simple or a shallow matter. God's salvation is the Triune God becoming a man, living a human life for thirty-three and a half years, dying an all-inclusive, all-terminating, all-redeeming, and all-releasing death, and accomplishing an all-producing resurrection. In such a condition and with such a situation, He ascended to the heavens to be made officially by God the Lord, the Christ, the Ruler of all the kings, and the Savior. Then He poured out Himself so that mankind could receive Him by calling on

Him (Acts 2:17-21). Many did receive Him. Immediately He, as the all-inclusive, compound Spirit, the consummation of the Triune God, entered into everyone who received Him.

Through the All-inclusive Redemption

In His salvation He has redeemed us from our sinfulness and has terminated us in our sinful constitution. Redemption, forgiveness, justification, and reconciliation are all included in His salvation. We were sinners and enemies toward God. We were sinners not merely by committing sins; we were sinners by constitution (Rom. 5:19; 2 Cor. 5:21). We became a constitution of sin and were the totality of sin. Thus, we needed not only to be forgiven but also to be terminated. Christ's death on the cross did a wonderful job of terminating our sinful constitution and taking away all our sinfulness. Based on such a death we have redemption and forgiveness, and as God's enemies we were reconciled to God. Now there is no contradiction between us and God; the situation between us and God has been altogether appeased. God is satisfied with the all-inclusive death of Christ, and this death also has satisfied us. Now we can thank Him for His all-inclusive death that has terminated our sinful constitution and has redeemed us from our sinfulness. Through such a redemption we have been forgiven, and God has justified us and even reconciled us, His enemies, to Himself. In such a situation the problem between us and God has been fully cleared up.

Unto the Dynamic Salvation of God

However, this is not all. Rather, at this juncture this dear One as the all-inclusive Spirit, who is the pneumatic Christ and the consummation of the Triune God, entered into us. Now we, the poor sinners and the enemies of God, have become such persons. The entire Triune God with all His processes has entered into us. This One is our Savior, our Lord, our Master, our God, our Father, and our all in all. Now He remains in us, abides in us (1 John 3:24b), lives in us (Gal. 2:20a), is being formed in us (4:19), and is making His home in our hearts (Eph. 3:17). Furthermore, He is transforming us and conforming us to His image (2 Cor. 3:18;

Rom. 8:29), making us the same as He is. Ultimately, He will glorify us with Himself as the glory (Col. 1:27).

In such a salvation, He is our everything and we are His expression. He and we, we and He, are one. We abide in Him and He abides in us (John 15:4a). We coinhere with Him: He lives in us and we live in Him. We and He are one person. Are we men or are we God? Actually, we are both. Are we divine or merely human? We are both; we are humanly divine and divinely human. We are human beings, and we are also divine beings. We are God-men. We are in the pneumatic Christ, who is the embodiment of the Triune God and the consummation of the Triune God. Not only so, the Triune God, Christ, and the consummated, compound Spirit are all in us. This is God's salvation.

We do not need to go to heaven. Heaven is within us. Heaven has come down to the earth. We do not love heaven, but we love the very Christ. Christ is much better than heaven. I assure you that where Christ is, heaven is there. We do not need to worry about heaven. We simply need to enjoy Christ. We are in heaven because we are in Christ. Christ is our heaven. Because of such a salvation, we are buoyant; we would never be down but would always be up.

Six thousand years ago God created man. He waited four thousand years, and then He became a man. Then, in the next two thousand years He made man one with Him practically. Today we are here as God-men. Hell is under our feet, and the lake of fire is far away. Because we are in Him, wherever He is, is heaven to us. He is buoyant, and we are buoyant in Him. Our sinful constitution has been terminated, and we have been redeemed from our sinfulness. Therefore, there is no problem between us and God. We have been justified by God and reconciled to God, and we are in an absolutely peaceful condition and situation with God. Based on this, we can enjoy Him, and He can flood into us to be our everything.

This is God's salvation, and this is the dynamic salvation. At times we may feel weak, dying, or even dead, but He is the resurrecting life (John 11:25). This resurrecting life counters our weakness and our deadness (2 Cor. 10:10). In ourselves we may become fatigued, weak, and dead; but He is in us as the resurrecting life. He resurrects us. This is God's salvation. God's salvation is nothing but God Himself making Himself our contents and making us a part of Him in the divine organic union. God's salvation is the saving God Himself plus His redemption. The redeeming and saving God Himself is our dynamic salvation. This is the heavenly view that we all need to see. With such a view, when we come to the Bible, it will become a new book to us.

Chapter Four

IN THE GROWTH OF THE BELIEVERS

Scripture Reading: John 3:5-6, 15; 1 Pet. 1:3, 23; James 1:18; Matt. 13:3; 1 John 3:9; Rev. 14:1-5, 14-16; 1 Cor. 3:6-7; 1 Pet. 2:2; Heb. 5:14; Col. 1:28; Eph. 4:15b, 11-13; Col. 2:19; Gal. 5:25, 16a; Rom. 8:4b; 1 Pet. 2:5; 1 Cor. 3:12

OUTLINE

I. Having been regenerated by the Spirit with the life of God as the seed contained in God's word—John 3:5-6, 15; 1 Pet. 1:3, 23; James 1:18; Matt. 13:3; 1 John 3:9.

II. Growing to be:
   A. The firstfruits as the overcomers—Rev. 14:1-5.
   B. The harvest ripened for reaping—Rev. 14:14-16.

III. Having been planted and watered for God to cause the growth—1 Cor. 3:6-7.

IV. Growing unto salvation by drinking the milk of the word—1 Pet. 2:2.

V. Growing unto maturity by eating the solid food—Heb. 5:14; Col. 1:28.

VI. Growing up into the Head, Christ, in all things—Eph. 4:15b.

VII. Growing unto the measure of the stature of the fullness of Christ by being perfected by the gifted persons—Eph. 4:11-13.

VIII. Growing with the growth of God—Col. 2:19.

IX. Growing by:
   A. Living by the Spirit—Gal. 5:25a.
   B. Walking by the Spirit—Gal. 5:16a, 25b.
   C. Having our being only according to the spirit—Rom. 8:4b.

X. Growing for the building up of the Body of Christ through transformation—Eph. 4:12b; 1 Pet. 2:2, 5; 1 Cor. 3:12.

In the previous three chapters we saw that God created man after His kind. He prepared a spirit within man that man might contact Him, receive Him, and contain Him by the way of taking God as his life. This is fully signified in the tree of life (Gen. 2:8-9). Eventually, God came to be a man. First, He created man; then He came to be a man in order to make man God in life and nature but not in the Godhead, not in the position and rank of God. Then He went to die, and He resurrected. In His resurrection He became a life-giving Spirit (1 Cor. 15:45b) that He might enter into our spirit to be one with us in this spirit (1 Cor. 6:17). Now He is within us so that day by day we may live Him, express Him, and magnify Him by walking and doing everything according to the Spirit (Phil. 1:20-21; Rom. 8:4; Gal. 5:16). This is wonderful, but still there is the need of something further: we need to grow. In order to grow, we need to know the way to grow and also the purpose for which we should grow.

HAVING BEEN REGENERATED BY THE SPIRIT WITH THE LIFE OF GOD AS THE SEED CONTAINED IN GOD'S WORD

In speaking concerning our growth in Christ, we must begin with regeneration. Our growth is based on the fact that we have been regenerated by the Spirit with the life of God as the seed contained in God's word (John 3:5-6, 15; 1 Pet. 1:3, 23; James 1:18; Matt. 13:3; 1 John 3:9). First, we were born in Adam through our parents; therefore, we have had one birth already. However, according to God's economy, every person should have another birth, a second birth; that is, every person should be regenerated. To be generated once is not adequate. We need to be regenerated—not to be born of our parents but to be born of God (John 1:12-13). We were born once of man, yet we need to be born a second time of God. Actually, we were created after God's kind, but that was not adequate. To be God's kind, we need God to be our life. This means that we need God to be our content.

When we believe in the Lord Jesus, the main thing is not that we are forgiven of our sins. Being forgiven of our sins is not the goal or the purpose. Being forgiven is merely the first step of the procedure to reach regeneration. Being redeemed, being forgiven of our sins, being justified by God, and being reconciled to God through Christ's redemption are four steps to reach the goal of regeneration.

Because we were sinners and even were the totality of sin with a sinful constitution, we needed God's forgiveness. The way for us to be forgiven by God is through Christ's redemption. Christ died a vicarious death for our sins (1 Cor. 15:3). Therefore, in Him, through Him, and with Him we have been redeemed (1 Pet. 1:18-19; Eph. 1:7). Based on Christ's redemption, God no longer condemns us but justifies us (Rom. 3:24). Now there is no problem between us and God. Then God reconciled us to Himself (2 Cor. 5:18; Rom. 5:10). Thus, our situation and condition before God have been fully appeased. We are now fully at peace with God (Rom. 5:1). However, although we have been redeemed, forgiven of our sins, justified by God, and reconciled to God so that we no longer have any problem with God, this is not the goal. Even though we may be thoroughly cleansed and purified, there still has been no change in our nature, substance, element, and essence. We are the same in essence as we were before. Our being dirty or clean does not change our inward essence. Whether dishes are washed or remain dirty, they are still dishes; their essence is not changed.

Hence, after redeeming us, forgiving us, justifying us, and reconciling us to Himself, God came in to regenerate us. This is not only the last step of God's salvation to us but also the goal, the aim, of salvation. However, this goal, this aim, has been almost fully neglected by most of today's Christians. As long as they have been forgiven, have peace, and eventually will go to heaven, many Christians are satisfied. As long as they have Christ as their righteousness and are justified, that is all that matters to them. It is true that we have been justified, but justification is not for justification. Justification is for something further (Rom. 5:18b and note 2). Redemption, forgiveness, justification, and reconciliation are all for one goal: regeneration. Ultimately and consummately, we need a new birth. We need to be reborn (John 3:3, 5). We not only need to be washed; we need to be reborn, to be remade, to be transformed in our nature. We were made of clay. Because of this, we are very "muddy." The more we wash something made of clay, the dirtier it gets. Likewise, the more we try to wash ourselves, the more we expose our dirtiness.

Instead of being merely washed, we need to be regenerated. We need to be born of another life, a divine life, a life in another category. We need to be born of God and with God. As believers in Christ, we have experienced such a divine birth. On the day we repented, when we called on the name of the Lord Jesus, something unconsciously entered into us. Although we did not expect this to happen, something was added into us. That something is actually not a thing but a person, the divine person. The very God, even the Triune God, the Father, the Son, and the Spirit, came into us (Eph. 4:6; Col. 1:27; John 14:17). We have another person in us as a threefold Being—the Triune God.

As believers in Christ, we are not alone. We do not live, walk, and have our being by ourselves. We do not rejoice or weep by ourselves. We are continually with one Person who is not outside of us but within us. When we are happy, He is happy. When we are sad, He is sad. When we weep, He washes away our tears. We have another One with us. This One is the Triune God, the One who was triune from eternity, who created man, who even became a man, who walked and lived on this earth for thirty-three and a half years, who went to die on the cross an all-inclusive death for us, and who resurrected to become the life-giving Spirit. Today this One is the life-giving Spirit within us. Through this Spirit we have been reborn, regenerated, in our spirit (John 3:6). The Spirit of God regenerated our spirit. Now these two have become one mingled spirit (1 Cor. 6:17).

We were regenerated by the Spirit with the life of God. When the Spirit regenerates our spirit, we receive God as life. The regenerating Spirit brought God into our spirit as our life. From that time we began to have two lives—our natural life from our parents, and our divine life, which is from God and is God. The life of God is the seed contained in God's holy word. Here we have four things: the Spirit, the life of God, the seed, and the word. This means that God Himself as life has been sown as a seed into us.

In regeneration the Holy Spirit sowed God as a life seed into our being. The Lord Jesus likened the natural being of man to a field. He said that He came to sow Himself as a seed, through the word, into this field (Matt. 13:3, 19a; Mark 4:3, 14). The Lord Jesus came as a life seed to sow Himself into our being. From the day that the Lord sowed Himself into us, we have been growing not only physically but also divinely and spiritually. This is the growth of the believers. In today's Christianity divine matters like these are not taught very much. Instead, much of the teaching in today's Christianity focuses on matters such as how to have a good married life and family life. This is a tragedy.

GROWING TO BE THE FIRSTFRUITS AS THE OVERCOMERS AND THE HARVEST RIPENED FOR REAPING

The Bible teaches us that when we believed in Christ, the Spirit, the consummated Spirit who is the life-giving Spirit and who is the pneumatic Christ, came to sow God as a life seed into us. On that day this life seed began to grow. Eventually, this life seed will grow to be the firstfruits as the overcomers in Revelation 14:1-5, and then the harvest ripened for reaping in Revelation 14:14-16. In a wheat field there are the firstfruits, those that ripen first. According to the Old Testament typology, the firstfruits were to be presented to God in His sanctuary for God's enjoyment (Lev. 23:10-11; Exo. 23:19). After the firstfruits there is the harvest. In Revelation 14 the firstfruits are mentioned at the beginning of the chapter, and the harvest follows near the end of the chapter. This is God's crop. God is the life seed sown into us, and we are the field. The seed and the field grow together. Without the seed, nothing can grow; but without the field, the earth, the seed cannot grow. Thus, in the growth of a seed two elements, the seed and the earth, meet together, mingle together, and grow together.

As believers in Christ, we should not be concerned about matters such as how to have a good marriage. If we want to have the best marriage, we must be regenerated, and we must grow in this divine seed. This divine seed is growing within us. Every day He is growing, first to grow in us to make us the firstfruits, the overcomers, who are signified by Zion in the Old Testament. Among the Old Testament types there is God's holy city, Jerusalem, which is common and general. Within this city there is a high peak called Zion (Psa. 2:6; 125:1). Zion is the highlight of Jerusalem. Today the church is the heavenly Jerusalem (Heb. 12:22), and the overcomers are Zion as the high peak, the highlight. If all the believers are common and general, the church will be merely Jerusalem without a high peak, without Zion. Such a situation is not beautiful. Jerusalem's beauty is with Zion. Zion is the beauty of the holy city (Psa. 48:2; 50:2). Likewise, the overcomers are the beauty of a local church. In each local church there must be a group of believers who ripen earlier to be the firstfruits. These believers are Zion in that church. Although it is wonderful to have the church in many localities, we like to see the beauty, the highlight, the high peak, the body of overcomers, in all the churches. Overcomers are what the Lord is after today. The Lord is after the overcomers to stand up, to ripen early.

HAVING BEEN PLANTED AND WATERED FOR GOD TO CAUSE THE GROWTH

There are two main ways to grow trees. One way is to sow a seed. If we sow the seed of a peach, a peach tree will grow up. The second way is to plant the sapling of a peach tree into the earth. This sapling will grow to be a peach tree. In the Bible it is the same. First, the Bible tells us that God has sown Himself into our spirit as the life seed to grow a tree, a miniature of the tree of life. The tree of life was unique in Genesis 2:9, but today the tree of life grows in all of us, causing each of us to be a small tree of life. As small trees of life, we need to grow. We, the believers in Christ, have all been regenerated by God sowing Himself into us as the life seed. From that day a life tree came out.

Then, in 1 Corinthians 3:6 Paul said, "I planted." At times we may say that we sow Christ into people through the preaching of the gospel. At other times we can also declare that we plant Christ into people. To plant a sapling into a field is a quicker way to grow a tree than to sow a seed. Paul planted Christ. In verses 6 and 7 he said, "I planted, Apollos watered, but God caused the growth. So then neither is he who plants anything nor he who waters, but God who causes the growth." Planting and watering are two steps for God to give the growth. If Paul would not plant and Apollos would not come to water, there would be no way for God to give the growth.

We need to be sowers and planters, sowing and planting Christ into many vacant sinners. Today there are many sinners who do not have Christ. They are empty, vacant, waiting for Christ to be either sown into them or planted into them. If we have some dear friends who are still not believers in Christ or are believers in Christ in name but not in reality, these kinds of friends may have a feeling of emptiness within them. They may feel that their living on this earth is empty and is vanity of vanities. If they would pray, "Lord Jesus, I do not want to be empty anymore. I want to take You; I want to receive You," immediately they would be filled by Christ as either a seed or a plant. Sometimes they will be blessed to receive Christ not only as a small seed, but as a large plant planted into their being. This will cause them to feel that they are filled with Christ. They will be happy and will tell others that they are no longer empty, but they now have something within them, that is, Christ. Now Christ is growing in them. Then some "Apollos" in the church will go once a week to water them. This watering plus the planting gives God an opportunity to grow in them.

When people have Christ, Christ will be their improvement. If they do not have Christ, they will have no improvement. I came to the United States in 1958. Since that time I have been observing how America has gone on. According to my observation, America is degrading. Today's America is different from the America of thirty-five years ago. America is degrading because it is short of Christ. What America needs today is not finance but Christ. America today is on the top in science, education, politics, and military strength. However, America is short of Christ. America needs to be on the top in Christ. We need to have more Christ. If every morning we will remain with Christ for fifteen minutes, we will receive the benefit. We will give Christ a way for His growth in us. The need of today's America is Christ—the practical Christ, the real Christ, the living Christ, the Christ either as the seed or the living plant sown or planted into us.

GROWING UNTO SALVATION BY DRINKING THE MILK OF THE WORD

First Peter 2:2 says, "As newborn babes, long for the guileless milk of the word in order that by it you may grow unto salvation." For our physical growth, we need to drink milk. Likewise, for our spiritual growth, we need to drink the divine milk from the Word. Every morning we need to drink a cup of milk from the Word. If you will do this, you will see the blessing. You will be healthy and will be a tree of life growing. This tree will bear fruit, and all the fruit will nourish your wife, your children, your grandchildren, your neighbors, your colleagues in your office, or your classmates in your school. You will become the tree of life to all the people in your community. Today, America needs this. America needs Christ to grow in the neighborhoods, in the schools, in the offices, and among the families and the in-laws.

We should not merely attend the church meetings; we need to grow that we may be a tree of life to nourish today's communities in America. I am very grateful to the Lord that I live in America. Here I have the full liberty to speak what I want to speak for the Lord. I am grateful for this, but whenever I look at today's situation, I am saddened because of the shortage of Christ. Needless to say with the unbelievers, even with the believers there is the shortage of Christ, the lacking of the growth of Christ.

Peter said that if we drink the milk of the word, we will grow unto salvation. We should not think that we are fully saved and have no need of any further salvation. Such a concept is wrong. We still need to be saved every day, even every minute, from our temper, from our sorrows, and from our anxiety. We need to be saved from many things. I am a quick person. It is easy for me to lose my temper. When I was young, my temper was a trouble to me. But later on I learned that I can be saved, and I have been saved through the drinking of the milk of the word. Drinking the milk of the word causes us to grow unto salvation from our anger, our temper, our anxiety, our worry, our fear, and our trembling. Every day we need a daily salvation. We need today's salvation in our daily walk.

GROWING UNTO MATURITY BY EATING THE SOLID FOOD

Among today's Christians it is difficult to find one who is mature. Many Christians are still childish. In their joking with one another we cannot sense God. Also, they are too free in having contact with the opposite sex. It is no wonder that there is fornication even among Christians. A sister should not speak lightly to a brother. For a female to speak lightly is to sell herself cheaply. A sister must keep her female dignity (1 Tim. 2:9-10). This female dignity protects her from many sinful things. Furthermore, in order to avoid falling into sin, a sister should not get too near a member of the opposite sex. Our need is to grow unto maturity, to be matured. Even one who is still a teenager in his physical age can be a mature believer in Christ. I have seen some young people like this.

We need to grow unto maturity to know God, to know the Bible, to know the church, and to know today's situation and condition in a mature way. We should not be childish. In order to grow unto maturity, we need to eat solid food (Heb. 5:14; Col. 1:28). Drinking milk is for babes. Every day we need to drink a cup of milk from the Word. We also need to take some solid food from the Word. In the Bible words such as "God so loved the world" (John 3:16) and "Husbands, love your wives" (Eph. 5:25) are like milk. In contrast, those portions of the Word concerning God's creation of man in His image and according to His likeness, His preparing a human spirit by breathing His breath of life into man's nostrils, and His putting man in front of the tree of life, a figure of God Himself as life, are solid, like diamond. Nevertheless, we need to eat these portions. We need spiritual teeth that can eat such solid food, and we also need a spiritual stomach to digest such words. We need to grow unto maturity by eating the solid food.

GROWING UP INTO THE HEAD, CHRIST, IN ALL THINGS

In Ephesians 4:15 Paul said, "But holding to truth in love, we may grow up into Him in all things, who is the Head, Christ." We need to grow up into the Head, Christ, in all things. Even in small matters such as getting our hair cut, combing our hair, and choosing a necktie, we need to do them in Christ. Certain sisters may take twenty minutes to comb their hair yet not spend two minutes to pray. This is a great loss. We need to grow up into Christ in all the small matters in our daily life.

We do not need to conduct ourselves in a certain way because we are forced to do so by outward regulations. We need to grow to the extent that we are in Christ. If we grow into Christ, when we comb our hair, we will comb it in Christ and with Christ. In combing our hair we may say, "Lord Jesus, I am with You; be with me in my combing my hair." Ephesians 4:15 says that we need to grow until we reach the level of being in Christ in all things—in shopping, in buying a pair of shoes, in spending our money, and even in choosing a pair of eyeglasses. It is a great thing to grow up into the Head, Christ, in all things.

GROWING UNTO THE MEASURE OF THE STATURE OF THE FULLNESS OF CHRIST BY BEING PERFECTED BY THE GIFTED PERSONS

According to Ephesians 4:11-13, we also need to grow unto the measure of the stature of the fullness of Christ by being perfected by the gifted persons. Every person has the stature of a human being, but verse 13 speaks of "the stature of the fullness of Christ." The stature of the fullness of Christ is the stature of the church (Eph. 1:22-23). The church as the Body of Christ has a stature, and this stature has a measure. We need to grow to match that measure. The church is "tall," yet we are still so "short." Therefore, our measure does not match the stature of the church. If this is the case, how could the church be built up? In a family, if the children do not grow but remain small, the family cannot be built up. Today it is difficult to realize the building up of the church, because most Christians have not grown but have remained infants (1 Cor. 3:1-2; Heb. 5:12). Among Christians we can see many opinions, criticisms, reasonings, and outbursts of temper. Today, who is mature? Very few have grown unto the measure of the stature of the proper church.

GROWING WITH THE GROWTH OF GOD

Colossians 2:19 says that we are growing with the growth of God. This verse indicates that our God who is living in us is growing. In Himself He does not need to grow, for in Himself He is perfect and complete. Yet in us He needs to grow. He has been within many of us for years, but we may not allow Him to grow. I have seen some children who were so small at their birth that they had to be put into an incubator. However, from the time of their birth they lived in a situation and environment which fit in with their growth in every aspect. As a result, they grew to be very strong. In the same way, we need to give God a situation and environment that are fitting for Him to grow in us.

The growth of a plant depends on the environment in which it is placed. A plant in the shade may grow and yet bear no blossoms, whereas the same kind of plant placed in the sunshine may grow and produce many blossoms. In order to grow properly, plants also need to be in an environment where there is water and fresh air. Do we give our God the adequate environment for Him to grow in us?

Shopping is a great temptation to the sisters. Many of the sisters like to read the newspaper on Saturday to see what is on sale. When they are considering whether or not to go shopping, something within them restricts them. At such a time they need to say, "Lord, thank You for Your restriction. I give You the opportunity to grow. I drop my shopping." If they would do this, Christ would grow in them. However, most of the time the sisters would not care for the Lord's inner restriction. Instead, they would still go shopping. That restricts the Lord from growing in them. In many things we have an inner restriction, but we do not listen to that restriction. Instead, we go our way. Going our own way is a restriction to the Lord's growth in us. Spending money loosely without any care for the Lord restricts God's growing within us. In everything we have to consider Him. We need to give Him the convenience and let Him have the liberty, the free way, to go on in us. If we do this, He will grow in us. He will become a "strong young man" in us (1 John 2:14b). We grow with the growth of God, and the growth of God simply means the increase of God. God is in us, but He is short of His increase in us because we do not provide adequate room, adequate space, for Him to grow.

GROWING BY:

Living by the Spirit

The believers grow by living by the Spirit (Gal. 5:25a). We should not live by our American or Chinese disposition. We all should live by the indwelling Spirit.

Walking by the Spirit

We must not only live but even walk in every step by the Spirit. In everything we need to walk by the Spirit (Gal. 5:16a, 25b).

Having Our Being Only according to the Spirit

We must live by the Spirit, walk by the Spirit, and have our being only according to the spirit (Rom. 8:4b). This is the way by which we grow. It is also the way by which we give our God the opportunity and the environment to grow in us. By these steps we give every convenience to our God to move within us. We give every inch within our being for Him to spread, to act, to move, and to operate. In such a situation, surely He will grow in us. In His growth we grow. Actually, His growth within us is our growth. The real growth of the believers is the very Triune God growing in them.

GROWING FOR THE BUILDING UP OF THE BODY OF CHRIST THROUGH TRANSFORMATION

Our growing is for the unique purpose of God, that is, the building up of the Body of Christ through transformation (Eph. 4:12b; 1 Pet. 2:2, 5; 1 Cor. 3:12). The first stanza of hymn #395 (*Hymns*) begins, "O Jesus Christ, grow Thou in me." We all need to pray, "Lord, grow in me." Two additional hymns, #548 and #750, concern the matter of transformation. The young people need to spend their time on their education, and the working ones need to have a job in order to make a living, but the goal is not merely for us to have a proper daily living. The goal of our living is the building up of the Body of Christ. We need to be built up.

To build a building requires every piece of material to be complete and perfect. If a piece of material has a defect, it is unsuitable for the building. We need to grow to be complete and perfect. Then we can be proper pieces of material for the building up of the Body of Christ in our locality. Many dear saints are always unhappy with their local church. They love the churches in other localities, but they do not like the church where they are. So, they move to another city. When they come to that city, they have a "honeymoon" for a short time. After the church honeymoon is over, they begin to complain about the church in that city. They think that the church in a different city might be good. So, they move there. After being there for two months, they begin again to be unhappy. Eventually, such persons may say that none of the local churches is good, but they love the Body of Christ. However, the Body of Christ that they love is "in the air"; it is not on the earth where they are.

To love the Body of Christ, we need to love our own local church in the place where we are. We should not be "church movers," moving from locality to locality according to our taste. We should simply love the church in which we are. It is not the church that is not lovely. Speaking honestly, it is we who are not lovely. We need to behave ourselves in a lovely way. To do this we need to grow. If we do not grow, we cannot be built up with others.

We should grow unto maturity. In Colossians 1:28-29 the

apostle Paul said that he labored, struggling according to God's operation in him, in order to present every man full-grown in Christ. In this verse he used the words *labor* and *struggling* to describe his endeavoring to present all the believers in Christ mature before God. We are laboring, struggling, and striving to have all the saints grow unto maturity. Then they will all be good for the building up of the Body of Christ.

If you will spend some time to pray over this chapter, I believe the Lord will bless you and grant you the adequate and abounding grace that you may grow unto maturity to be good for the building up of the Body of Christ.

Chapter Five

IN THE BUILDING UP OF THE BODY OF CHRIST

Scripture Reading: Eph. 1:22-23; Rom. 12:5; Eph. 4:15-16; Col. 2:19; Eph. 4:12; 1 Cor. 3:12; Eph. 3:9; 1:10

OUTLINE

I. The Body of Christ, as the church of God, being an organism like the human body—Eph. 1:22-23:
   A. Constituted with all the living members of Christ—Rom. 12:5.
   B. Needing to grow for its building up.

II. The growth of the Body of Christ:
   A. Through the members growing into the Head, Christ, in all things by holding to truth in love—Eph. 4:15.
   B. Out from the Head, Christ, all the Body causes its growth—Eph. 4:16.
   C. With the growth of God—Col. 2:19b.

III. The building up of the Body of Christ:
   A. By the Body's growth:
      1. By its members being perfected to do the work of the New Testament ministry—the building up of the Body of Christ—Eph. 4:12.
      2. In the life of God—Col. 2:19.
      3. In the process of transformation—1 Cor. 3:12.
   B. By the building up of itself:
      1. By being joined together through every joint of the rich supply—Eph. 4:16b.
      2. By being knit together through the operation in the measure of each one part—Eph. 4:16b.
      3. In love—Eph. 4:16c.

IV. The fulfillment of the eternal economy of God—Eph. 3:9; 1:10:
   A. By carrying out the New Testament ministry—Eph. 4:12.
   B. To complete the building up of the church for the consummation of the New Jerusalem.

The subject of this chapter is the building up of the Body of Christ. Growth is one thing; building up is another. It seems that growth is mainly for the individual believer and that the building up is something corporate. However, we should not consider this to be true absolutely. Strictly speaking, growth is for the building, and growth equals the building. In the physical realm there are two kinds of building up. One is by putting pieces of material, such as wood or stone, together to form a building. This is a building by lifeless materials.

We also use the word *build* in reference to our physical bodies. This kind of building does not take place by putting lifeless pieces of material together. In this kind of building, the physical body is built up organically by growth. When an infant is built up to be a young boy of thirteen years of age, he is built up not by having things added to him. Rather, he is built up by growth organically. Our eyes, ears, and teeth were not built into our body by the addition of lifeless materials. They are present at birth, and they grow in a gradual way organically.

The building of the church as the Body of Christ is organic, by the growth in life. The Body of Christ is like our physical body. It is built up by its growth. Ephesians 4:15 says, "But holding to truth in love, we may grow up into Him in all things, who is the Head, Christ." Then verse 16 says, "Out from whom all the Body, being joined together and being knit together through every joint of the rich supply and through the operation in the measure of each one part, causes the growth of the Body unto the building up of itself in love." First, we must grow up into the Head in all things. Then from the Head something will come out to cause the growth of the Body. By this growth of the Body, the Body builds itself up in love. Growth equals building. The Body builds itself up by growing. This growth of the Body is not for any particular member. The Body grows for the entire Body.

In the recent rebellion in the Lord's recovery a teaching was promoted which said that all the local churches are autonomous. Immediately I recognized this as the wrong teaching of G. H. Lang, a teacher who was once among the Brethren. In correcting this wrong teaching I posed the question: "Can any part of our body be autonomous? Can the arm say that it is autonomous from the rest of the body?" The obvious answer is no. Any member of our body that decides to become autonomous will die. The members of the body are not autonomous.

Apparently, growth is for individual believers and building is corporate. Actually, both growth and building are corporate. The feet do not grow at one time, and the hands at a later time, as if the two were autonomous. The entire body grows together as a corporate entity. Therefore, the teaching concerning autonomy is nonsensical. Many years ago we discarded this teaching. There is no such thing as autonomy in the Body. Some in the recent rebellion taught autonomy in order to keep others away. They said, "Don't come to our place to bother us. We are a local church. We have our own jurisdiction. No one has any right to touch us." If this is true, where is the Body?

The Lord has made it clear to us that the building is the growth. Yes, growth is for the building, but building and growth are not two different things. As human beings, if we do not grow, we can never build ourselves up. In order to be built up, we need to grow every day and even every moment. It seems that this growth is so slow that we cannot tell any difference from day to day. However, after fifteen years, a small babe is built up to be a strong young man. This takes place not by addition but by growth.

Few Christians today know what the genuine building is. Therefore, it is easy to understand why, on the earth today, there is very little building among the children of God. In order to realize what building is, we must look at our physical body. Not one member of our body is separate. All the members stay together and grow together as a complete body.

THE BODY OF CHRIST, AS THE CHURCH OF GOD, BEING AN ORGANISM LIKE THE HUMAN BODY

The Body of Christ, as the church of God, is an organism like the human body (Eph. 1:22-23). The difference between an organism and an organization is life. A table is an organization with pieces of wood joined to other pieces. At first all the material for a table may be piled in one place without any organization. But when the craftsman puts the pieces together, he organizes them into a table. A table is an organization, but a man is an organism. As an organism, every man was conceived as a child in his mother's womb and remained there for nine months before being born out of that womb. The various parts of a child's body are not added to him along the way; they are already present and develop by the organic growth of his body. Thus, a man is altogether an organism, not an organization.

The Body of Christ is an organism. Thus, when believers, the constituents of the Body, do not live Christ, the church cannot be built up. Today there are many different kinds of Christian groups, but among these groups we cannot see one organism. Strictly speaking, even among us it is difficult to see a proper organism. What I have seen is mostly organization. Today among Christians, organizations are mushrooming. It seems that to begin a so-called church is easier than setting up a restaurant. There are street churches, home churches, state churches—all kinds of organizations. This is not the Body, because the Body is organic. As believers, we all have Christ in us, but we must live Christ. As we all live Christ, an organism is produced. The aggregate, the totality, of this kind of living of Christ is an organism, the Body of Christ.

Constituted with All the Living Members of Christ

The Body of Christ is not only built but is constituted with all the living members of Christ (Rom. 12:5).

Needing to Grow for Its Building Up

If we do not grow, there can be no building up of the Body of Christ. The building of the Body of Christ depends absolutely on our growth. We grow in the growth of God within us (Col. 2:19). When He grows in us, we grow in His growth, and this growth is the building up of the Body. Today Christians easily come together, and they are also easily scattered. At first they are happy to come together, but after a while they begin to be unhappy with each other. Eventually, they separate from one another, and in some cases they become enemies.

Our eyes need to be opened and enlightened to the revelation in the Bible, especially in the New Testament, concerning the church as the Body of Christ. According to this revelation, the church as the Body of Christ is altogether a matter of life. First, it must be born of God. Then it must grow, and by growing it builds itself up. The growth is organic, and the building is even more organic. It is not organic in us, because we are not organic, but it is organic in God. Plants themselves are organic, but the soil in which they grow is not organic. Even the nutrients of the soil are not organic. Being organic is a matter on the side of life. The church as the Body of Christ is organic on the life side, that is, on the side of God. Before we were regenerated, we did not have God. Today, however, we have God. Through regeneration God has been born into our being. Hence, we not only have God added into us; we also have God born into us organically. From the time of regeneration we have an organic union with Him.

THE GROWTH OF THE BODY OF CHRIST

Through the Members Growing into the Head, Christ, in All Things by Holding to Truth in Love

The growth of the Body of Christ is through the members growing into the Head, Christ, in all things by holding to truth in love (Eph. 4:15). We, the members of Christ, must grow into the Head. We can be a Christian, a member of Christ, and yet have many aspects in which we are not in Christ. Our gossiping, our reasoning, our murmuring, and our arguing are all outside of Christ.

It is difficult to deal with the young people concerning their talking on the telephone. If their parents ask them to do something, they may say, "I have no time. I am busy." After a short time the telephone may ring, and one of them may answer it. After a while one of the parents may inform this one that he needs to use the telephone. The young one may respond by saying that he will be on the telephone for only another five minutes. Eventually, five minutes turns into fifty minutes. Is that kind of talking on the telephone in

Christ? We all need to grow into Christ, particularly in the matter of using the telephone. I am the same as you are. I like to talk to people on the telephone. But while I am speaking on the telephone, my Partner within me often says, "It is sufficient. Stop." This word *stop* is continually being spoken within me while I am speaking. My response to the One within me is: "Just one more minute." But my Partner continues to say, "Stop." After such a telephone call, I need ten minutes to make a confession: "Lord, forgive me. I deliberately sinned against You. You were within me stopping me, checking with me, but I would not listen. I lied to You more than ten times by saying that I would stop in just one minute, but I did not keep my word. What a sinner I am! Lord, forgive me." Such a confession could not easily be forgotten. Thereafter, if another telephone call comes, I am fearful and even trembling that I may speak too much. In this way I learned the lesson of growing, particularly in the matter of handling telephone calls.

We also need to consider the matters of gossiping, reasoning, and murmuring. Each day how much time do we spend gossiping? Some saints are very free in passing on information about others. Too much time has been wasted and too many dollars have been spent in talking vainly on the telephone. In such activities we have been outside of Christ. In this kind of situation it is impossible to have the building up of the Body of Christ. We need the building up in Christ and the building up into the Body of Christ.

Very often I do not have the freedom to speak certain things even to my wife. The One who restricts me is my Partner, Christ, who is within me. I do not have the freedom to tell my wife everything. If I tell my wife some unnecessary thing, my talk becomes gossip. This question rises up within me when I speak to my wife about another brother: "Why do you have to tell your wife about this brother? Is it for shepherding or for taking care of the saints?" If it is for shepherding, it may be all right. But quite often the matter of shepherding is used as an excuse, a covering. Our appetite may not be for shepherding or taking care of the saints; rather, our taste may be to talk about others. We may even tell our wife to keep something we have said about another brother confidential, yet we must realize that such a saying cannot be kept confidential. If we had not given the charge of confidentiality to our wife, she might have been slow to tell others. But because of our charge, what we have said will be spread to various places. Eventually, I learned the lesson: To grow into Christ, do not speak about others. In the church life, the saints' gossiping, reasoning, and debating have wasted much time and money. Concerning the vital groups, we have charged the saints to go out to visit people two hours a week. To budget two hours every week to go out may seem to be very difficult. But if we add together all the time spent on the telephone in one week, we may discover that we have spent more than two hours on the telephone.

My burden is not to minister doctrines to the saints. My desire is to transfuse you with the very Christ whom I have experienced. When I am on the telephone, He is in me. As I am talking to the other party, He is instructing me within. Then after the telephone conversation, many times I have to kneel down to confess to Him. This is my real experience of Christ.

According to Ephesians 4:15, the members of the Body grow up into Christ in all things by holding to truth in love. In this verse the word *truth* refers to anything that is real. By this word alone I have learned that many telephone calls are not true. There is much vain talk on the telephone. Such talk is vanity, not truth. What is truth? God is truth, Christ is truth, the Spirit is truth, the divine life is truth, the Body of Christ is truth, the gospel is truth, and salvation is truth. By holding to these true things, we grow into Christ. If we hold to these real things, we are actually growing into the Head, Christ, in all things. Otherwise, we are not growing into Christ.

Dear saints, if this word impresses you and you take it, practice it, and live it, you will receive much blessing. It will save you time and energy. Instead of speaking vainly about others, it is better for you to shut your eyes and sit down to rest awhile in the Lord. The amount of time you spend talking vanity can be used to sit before the Lord. You do not even need to speak to the Lord; just sit with Him and rest. If you try this, you will have the real growth into the Head in all things, by holding to truth in love.

The phrase *in love* is very meaningful. When we speak something to others in vanity, this indicates that we do not love the Lord and we do not love the one of whom we are speaking. We do not have the right to expose others, but we still expose them. Instead of exposing others' mistakes, we should cover them, not telling anyone about them. This is love (1 Pet. 4:8). Yet we are just the opposite. We like to tell people about others, exposing them to others. To inform is not to love. To love is to cover others' shortcomings and weaknesses. To talk in vanity to everyone indicates that we do not love the church. The church has been damaged very much by this kind of exposing. If everyone in a church refrains from exposing others and is full of prayers, singing, and praises to the Lord, that church is beautiful.

Out from the Head, Christ, All the Body Causes Its Growth

After growing up into Christ, the Head, in all things, we will surely remain in the Head. Then, out from the Head, Christ, all the Body will cause its growth (Eph. 4:16).

Suppose that during the day we all live loosely, telling stories to one another. We all need to realize that this kind of storytelling brings death to us. In the evening when the time of meeting comes, we all will come and sit down in a deadened condition. If everyone is dead, the meeting also will be a dead meeting. There will be no singing, praising, or giving of thanks, because all were killed during the day. But suppose there is no such storytelling and no gossiping, reasoning, or debating in the church. This situation will keep everyone in a living condition with praising and singing to the Lord. Then when we come to the meeting, the meeting will be uplifted, high, full of the Spirit, full of singing, and full of Amens.

Because all the attendants in the meeting are deadened, sometimes it is difficult for the speakers to begin the meeting. The deadening atmosphere is in the meeting because the church has been deadened. Yet many do not have any consciousness of the deadness. They do not feel that they have done anything wrong, yet they have been so free to expose others. This might be the reason that we have been in one city meeting regularly week by week for ten years and yet have very little building. We need to hold to truth and allow no vanity to come out of our mouths (Eph. 4:29). Then we will maintain a living atmosphere, and whenever we come together, we will be very living, organic, full of praises, full of thanks, and full of prayers. Everyone will be able to pray and everyone will be able to open his mouth.

If we are living, when we open our mouth, our prayer also becomes living. But if we are deadened, even though we may struggle to pray, "Lord, I thank You. Lord, You are so good," there is still nothing but deadening. Even our prayer is deadening. This kind of deadening affects the ministers of the word. Eventually, the church is annulled. The reality of the church is taken away by our looseness, carelessness, and vanity in different matters. As a result, we do not have the growth, and without growth, building is impossible. The building up of the Body of Christ should not be merely a term on our lips; it should be something carried out in our daily life that builds up. That is building up by growth, and that is to grow up for the building up.

With the Growth of God

Be assured that when we live in the way of holding to truth in love, God will always be added into our being. Colossians 2:19 says that the Body "grows with the growth of God." In Himself God does not need to grow; He is altogether complete and perfect. But in us, He needs to grow. The measure of Christ in us is too short, and the quantity of Christ is too little. We need more Christ. We need God to be increased within us. We grow with this kind of growth.

THE BUILDING UP OF THE BODY OF CHRIST

By the Body's Growth

The building up of the Body of Christ is by the Body's

growth. We all need to grow that the Body may be built up. If we grow, the Body grows, and the Body grows for its building up.

By Its Members Being Perfected to Do the Work of the New Testament Ministry—the Building Up of the Body of Christ

The growth of the Body is by the Body's members being perfected to do the work of the New Testament ministry—the building up of the Body of Christ (Eph. 4:12). Not only in Christianity but also among us, very often the saints cannot function in the meetings. The reason for this is that we are short of growth. If we are growing day by day, we will be living. Then when we come to the meetings, either we will offer a prayer or we will say, "Praise the Lord!" This indicates that we are living. But today's situation is for the most part not like this. I have attended prayer meetings where the saints and even the leading ones came in five, ten, or fifteen minutes after the scheduled time. As a result, the entire meeting was deadened. It is impossible for a church in this condition to be built up. We all need to be living, to be growing, day by day. Then the whole church will grow, and this growth equals the building.

Through the growth of the Body all the members are perfected to do the work of the New Testament ministry. This work is done not by the apostles, prophets, evangelists, or shepherd-teachers, but by the ordinary, common members of the Body of Christ. When each member is perfected to do the work of the New Testament ministry, all the members will know how to build up the Body. The building up is the New Testament work. If all the saints are carrying out the work of the ministry, the meetings will become living, and we will escape the deadened situation of today's Christianity.

In the Life of God

The building up of the Body is by the Body's growth in the life of God (Col. 2:19). Therefore, it is organic.

In the Process of Transformation

The building up of the Body also takes place in the process of transformation (1 Cor. 3:12). Today as we are growing, we are in the process of transformation. Spontaneously, we are being transformed. To be transformed is not to change, to adjust ourselves, or to correct ourselves. These are mere outward changes. Transformation is metabolic, something within in life.

During every meal as we take food into our stomach, digestion, a metabolic process, immediately begins to take place. For the stomach to move metabolically, it must be filled with some element. I have experienced this metabolic process in eating many times. One day after speaking in a meeting, I was physically exhausted. Twenty minutes after eating some food, I was vitalized. A metabolic process had begun to go on within me. After another ten minutes, I was even more vitalized. I was not only vitalized; I was transformed by the metabolic process within me. This is an illustration of transformation. We need to grow that we may be transformed. After being transformed, we are suitable for the building up of the Body of Christ.

By the Building Up of Itself

Ephesians 4:16 says that the Body grows unto the building up of itself. This means that the growth of the Body is the Body's building up of itself.

By Being Joined Together through Every Joint of the Rich Supply

The Body builds up itself by being joined together through every joint of the rich supply (Eph. 4:16b). These joints of the rich supply are the gifted persons, as mentioned in Ephesians 4:11: the apostles, prophets, evangelists, and shepherds and teachers. These gifted persons are rich joints, full of Christ as the life supply. They are a factor to join the saints together. This is the first kind of joining together.

By Being Knit Together through the Operation in the Measure of Each One Part

The Body builds up itself also by being knit together through the operation in the measure of each one part (Eph. 4:16b). This is the second kind of joining. The first kind of joining, the joining through the joints of the rich supply, is like putting pieces together to form the frame of a building. After framing a building, there are many openings that need to be filled. The second kind of joining, the knitting together through the operation of each one part, is like filling in all the openings after a building has been framed. Knitting is to interweave until all the openings are filled up by the interwoven pieces.

The parts of the Body that are knit, or interwoven, together are not the gifted persons but the common members of the Body. The gifted persons are joined together to form the frame; the common parts function in their measure to be knit and interwoven in order to fill up all the holes. This is not merely a doctrine; I have practiced this, I saw this, and I experienced this. It is possible. If you have the heart, pray to the Lord: "Lord, have mercy upon me and grant me the adequate grace. I want to live You organically." Then go and meet together with the saints in your place. There may be a number of other saints who are the same as you are. As you meet together there will be a growth among you. This growth equals the building. Some gifted persons will be joined together to form the frame, and the rest will do their part by functioning in their measure. In this way the church is built up.

In Love

The Body of Christ also builds up itself in love (Eph. 4:16c). The little phrase *in love* is used in the book of Ephesians six times (1:4; 3:17; 4:2, 15, 16; 5:2). God chose us in eternity in love (1:4). His predestinating us unto sonship in eternity past was also in love (v. 5). Without love God would not have chosen or predestinated us. Today we need to grow in love, and we also need to build up the Body in love. We love the Lord, we love the church, and we love every member. Regardless of how weak certain members may be, or even how evil they may be, we love them because they are members. Our attitude should be that we do not like to expose them. We desire instead to cover them in love. This is growth and this is building.

THE FULFILLMENT OF THE ETERNAL ECONOMY OF GOD

The building up of the Body of Christ will usher in the fulfillment of the eternal economy of God. God's eternal economy is referred to by the apostle Paul in Ephesians 1 and 3. In Ephesians 3:9-10 Paul said, "And to enlighten all that they may see what the economy of the mystery is…in order that now to the rulers and the authorities in the heavenlies the multifarious wisdom of God might be made known through the church." In Ephesians 1:10 Paul said that the church carries out the economy of God that all things can be headed up in Christ. Today the whole universe is in a state of collapse. But, since the church will be headed up in Christ, the church will be used by Christ to head up all things in the universe in Christ. This is to fulfill God's economy.

By Carrying Out the New Testament Ministry

In the building up of the Body of Christ, the fulfillment of the eternal economy of God is accomplished by carrying out the New Testament ministry (Eph. 4:12).

To Complete the Building Up of the Church for the Consummation of the New Jerusalem

By the carrying out of the New Testament ministry, the building up of the church will be completed for the consummation of the New Jerusalem. The built-up church will usher in the New Testament consummation, the New Jerusalem, to fulfill God's economy.

THE ORGANIC CONSTITUTION OF THE CHURCH AS THE BODY OF CHRIST

We all have to realize that the church as the Body of Christ is an organism, an organic constitution constituted with divinity plus humanity. Ephesians 4:4-6 says, "One Body and one Spirit...one Lord...one God and Father of all." The church is the Body; this is the human frame, on the human side. In this frame there is the Divine Trinity as the divine constituent for the Body's constitution. The Spirit is the essence of the Body, the Lord is the element, and God the Father is the source. From the source the element comes, and within the element is the essence. This essence is the Spirit. The church as an organism is constituted on the human side as a frame and on the divine side as the contents. The divine essence, element, and source are mingled with the human frame. The church is such an organism. This is what God is after today, and this is according to God's desire. God is expecting to have this, but there is not such a thing on this earth today. Yet, we must believe that if we are faithful to all that is revealed in this book, such a thing will take place on this earth as a testimony of God Himself and as a declaration against God's enemy, Satan. May the Lord have mercy on us and grant us the grace we need, so that such a wonderful building can be seen on the earth today.

Hymn #840 (*Hymns*) is a very practical song concerning the building up of the Body of Christ.

1 Freed from self and Adam's nature,
Lord, I would be built by Thee
With the saints into Thy temple,
Where Thy glory we shall see.
From peculiar traits deliver,
From my independent ways,
That a dwelling place for Thee, Lord,
We will be thru all our days.

2 By Thy life and by its flowing
I can grow and be transformed,
With the saints coordinated,
Builded up, to Thee conformed;

Keep the order in the Body,
 There to function in Thy will,
Ever serving, helping others,
 All Thy purpose to fulfill.

3 In my knowledge and experience
 I would not exalted be,
But submitting and accepting
 Let the Body balance me;
Holding fast the Head, and growing
 With His increase, in His way,
By the joints and bands supplying,
 Knit together day by day.

4 By Thy Spirit daily strengthened
 In the inner man with might,
I would know Thy love surpassing,
 Know Thy breadth and length and height;
Ever of Thy riches taking,
 Unto all Thy fulness filled,
Ever growing into manhood,
 That Thy Body Thou may build.

5 In God's house and in Thy Body
 Builded up I long to be,
That within this corporate vessel
 All shall then Thy glory see;
That Thy Bride, the glorious city,
 May appear upon the earth,
As a lampstand brightly beaming
 To express to all Thy worth.

Chapter Six

IN THE CONSUMMATION OF THE NEW JERUSALEM

Scripture Reading: 2 Pet. 3:10-12; Rev. 21:1; 22:1; 21:6; 22:17b; John 4:14; 7:37-39; Rev. 22:2, 14; 2:7; 21:3, 22, 11

OUTLINE

I. The New Jerusalem being the consummation of all the works of God's new creation out of His old creation in all the dispensations through the ages, including:
   A. The ages in the Old Testament:
      1. The age before the law, from Adam to Moses.
      2. The age of the law, from Moses to Christ's first coming.
   B. The ages in the New Testament:
      1. The age of grace, from Christ's first coming to His second coming.
      2. The age of the kingdom, from Christ's second coming to the end of the old creation (2 Pet. 3:10-12; Rev. 21:1).

II. The New Jerusalem being the aggregate of God's organic union and mingling with His redeemed, regenerated, transformed, and glorified people:
   A. The constitution of God as life in the redeemed humanity.
   B. The organic building of divinity with humanity.
   C. With the processed Triune God to be the flowing river of water of life as the very center and the very source of supply of the holy city—Rev. 22:1:
      1. To quench organically the thirst of God's people mingled and built together with God for eternity—Rev. 21:6; 22:17b; cf. John 4:14; 7:37-39.

2. To satisfy organically the entire city with Christ as the tree of life growing in the river of water of life for eternity—Rev. 22:2, 14; 2:7.

III. The New Jerusalem being God's ultimate organism:
   A. For the redeeming God to dwell organically in His redeemed people as His tabernacle for eternity—Rev. 21:3.
   B. For God's redeemed people to dwell organically in their redeeming God as their temple for eternity—Rev. 21:22.
   C. As the processed Triune God's eternal manifestation and expression:
      1. With the processed Triune God as the glory of its content—Rev. 21:11a.
      2. With the conformed people as the shining light of its appearance—Rev. 21:11b.
      3. The ultimate issue of the organic union in God's relationship with man in His life which is unsearchably rich in eternity.

THE TREE OF LIFE BEING THE CENTER OF THE BIBLE

The Bible is the holy Word, God's oracle. It is an oracle full of divine revelations. First, it unveils God to us. Genesis 1:1 says, "In the beginning God created." Divinely speaking, the Bible is a book of revelation. Humanly speaking, to us it is a storybook containing the story concerning God. This story has a center. The center in this story is the tree of life (Gen. 2:8-9). This story unveils God to us, but the center of the story is the tree of life.

At the beginning of the Bible a very striking, particular, and peculiar tree, the tree of life, is standing there. Perhaps we have seen hundreds of kinds of trees, but we have never seen a tree named *life*. The Bible as a storybook begins with this tree and ends with this tree (Rev. 22:1-2). This tree is the center of the whole world. Some maps of the world place the Mediterranean Sea, with the small nation of Israel on its eastern shore, at the center of the populated world. The Garden of Eden was not far from today's Israel. Genesis 2 tells us that where the tree of life was, there was a river with four heads, one of which was the Euphrates (v. 14). That is the river where Babylon was built. Today's Iraq is on the Euphrates. The Euphrates is one of the four heads of the particular river that flowed out of Eden to water the garden where the tree of life was. This means that the tree of life is at the center of the populated earth. Then, at the end of the Bible there is a holy city. In the center of that city is God's throne (Rev. 22:1, 3). Out of the throne flows the river of water of life, and along this river, on its two sides, grows the tree of life, not like a pine shooting upward, but as a vine spreading forward to reach every part of the city until it reaches the twelve gates (vv. 1-2). This indicates that this nourishing tree is the center of the entire New Jerusalem. The story of the Bible is that God made the tree of life the center.

Now we need to ask, "What is the tree of life?" or "Who is the tree of life?" As I have pointed out in previous chapters, God became incarnated to be a man. After this man grew up to be thirty years of age, He came out to minister. In His ministry, one day He told people, "I am…the life" (John 14:6). This sentence is short and the words are simple enough for a preschool child to read: I am the life. In the next chapter, John 15, He said, "I am the true vine" (v. 1). These two sentences put together equal "I am the life tree." Therefore, the tree of life, the life tree, is Christ. We need to be bold to say that Christ, who is the embodiment of the Triune God (Col. 2:9), is a tree, a vine tree, and this vine tree is the tree of life.

In Genesis 2:9 there is no indication or hint that the tree of life was a vine. However, when we come to the end of the Bible, we find that the tree of life is a vine. We know this because it grows not by shooting upward but by spreading out to reach people. It is one tree, but it grows on two sides of the river. Hence, it must be a vine. Between Genesis and Revelation there is another chapter of the Bible concerning Christ—John 15—in which He told us that He is the true vine. There are many vines on this earth, but only one vine is true. This vine is Christ.

The queen of England has a large vine. In 1958 I was invited to England, and while I stayed there some brothers brought me to see the Queen's vine, a large vine in a glass room. The British people were boasting of that tree. When they asked me what I thought about it, I replied that the Queen's vine was too small compared with the true vine that I had seen. The Queen's vine had not yet filled the room where it was kept, but the vine that I had seen had circled the entire globe many times. No one can measure its length. Christ, the great vine tree, is everywhere on this globe. He is in Seattle, in Hong Kong, in New York, in New Zealand—in every place on this earth. Therefore, we should not listen to some Bible teachers who say that there is no tree of life today. That is a falsehood. The tree of life is here today.

Like God Himself, the things concerning God are mysterious and abstract. It is difficult to describe such an abstract and mysterious God. Therefore, God used the wisest way to teach us concerning Himself. He taught us like a teacher in a kindergarten. A kindergarten teacher teaches her students by means of pictures. There is a saying that a picture is better than a thousand words. Thus, in Genesis 2 God set forth a picture, the tree of life. We might say that after this picture appeared in the Old Testament, it disappeared for a while. In the Old Testament we cannot see the picture of the tree of life after Genesis 3, because due to the fall of man, the way to the tree of life was closed by the cherubim, signifying God's glory, and also by the flaming sword, the flame signifying God's holiness and the sword signifying God's righteousness (3:24). This indicates that to the fallen mankind the way to the tree of life was closed by God's glory, God's holiness, and God's righteousness. There was no longer an entrance for fallen mankind to touch the tree of life.

But one day God Himself came out of eternity and entered into time to be a man. Then He died on the cross for the man whom He had created and who had become fallen. He died an all-inclusive death, which was also a vicarious death. By that death He satisfied the demands of God's glory, God's holiness, and God's righteousness. In a sense, He took away the cherubim and the flaming sword, so that the closed entrance was opened again. Hebrews 10:19-20 says that a new and living way has been initiated for us to come to God as the tree of life. Actually, in this new way we do not need to go to the tree of life; the tree of life came to us and is now with us. He was with Peter and John, and He was so close that John could even lie in His bosom. Then this One opened His mouth and told them, "I am the life" and "I am the true vine." This means that He is the tree of life to His believers. Every day His disciples were dealing with the tree of life, yet they did not know it. They were dealing with the tree of life without being conscious of it.

THE NEW JERUSALEM BEING THE CONCLUSION OF THE BIBLE

This long storybook, the Bible, does have a conclusion. This conclusion is the New Jerusalem (Rev. 21:9—22:3). If we were to ask some careful pastors, "What is the New Jerusalem?" they might advise us not to touch this matter. They might also advise us not to touch the entire book of Revelation, in which the New Jerusalem is mentioned, because

Revelation is a mystery. On the other hand, some careless pastors might say that the New Jerusalem is a heavenly mansion that Christ is building for us in heaven. They would say that the Lord Jesus told us in John 14 that He would build such a mansion for us, in which there is a room for every believer in Christ. If we do believe in Christ, when we die, we will go there to enjoy the eternal life, which equals the eternal blessings. When I was a young Christian I believed such teaching, but later I discarded it.

Its Construction

The New Jerusalem has three sections. The city proper, or the city itself, is pure gold (21:18b). This means that the base of the city is gold. The second part of the city is its twelve gates, each of which is a pearl (vv. 12-13, 21). The third part of the city is the wall with its foundations, all of which are precious stones (vv. 14, 18a, 19-20). The entire wall is jasper, and the foundation of the wall has twelve layers. The first layer of the foundation also is jasper. Revelation 4:2-3a tells us that God's appearance is like jasper. Thus, in appearance the city is exactly the same as God. God appears like jasper, and the city also appears like jasper.

The three sections of the New Jerusalem are constructed with three kinds of materials, or three kinds of elements. The number *three* is a particular number in the universe, signifying the Triune God. The Triune God is the number *three*. Every number in the Bible has its meaning, and *three* signifies the Triune God. Therefore, the three kinds of materials in the New Jerusalem no doubt signify the Triune God.

The first material is gold, which constitutes the city proper and forms the base of the city. In the Bible gold refers to God the Father as the base, the fountain, the source. The second material is pearl. Pearls are produced by oysters, and oysters live in the sea, signifying the death water. One day a small rock enters into an oyster and wounds it. This rock then remains in the wound, and the oyster secretes its life juice from the wound around the rock, layer after layer. Eventually, a pearl is produced. This indicates that Christ is the living "oyster." He lived in the death water, the world. One day we sinners as small "rocks" wounded Him. He was wounded by us and for us, and He retained us in His wound. Through His death we were redeemed, and His death also released His divine life (John 12:24), the life juice of the "oyster." His resurrection secretes the divine life around the redeemed sinners to make them all pearls. These pearls become the entrance to the holy city.

Christ's redemption with His secretion in the resurrection life first redeemed us and then secreted the divine life around us, making us pearls. Through Christ's resurrection we were regenerated (1 Pet. 1:3), and regeneration is the very entrance into the kingdom of God (John 3:5). In the New Jerusalem God the Father is signified by the gold, and God the Son, by the pearls. By making us pearls, God the Son has now become us. Both Christ and we are pearls. Here we can see the organic union. The organic union indicates that Christ is united with us organically through His death and resurrection. His death becomes the redeeming death, and His resurrection becomes the secreting resurrection. He redeemed us, and He secretes His life juice over us to make us pearls, which are both He and we. In this way the second person of the Trinity became us. This is the organic union.

The twelve gates of pearl bear the names of the twelve tribes of Israel (Rev. 21:12). This indicates that these pearls are the twelve tribes of Israel. A name always denotes the person who bears that name. Therefore, the twelve pearls must be the twelve tribes of Israel. The twelve foundations of precious stones bear the names of the twelve apostles (v. 14). The twelve tribes represent the Old Testament saints, and the twelve apostles represent the New Testament saints. Although we are common believers, we are the saints. Initially, we, the saints, were pieces of clay; we were made of dust (Gen. 2:7). Eventually, through transformation by the Spirit this clay becomes precious stones (1 Cor. 3:12b; 2 Cor. 3:18; 1 Pet. 2:5). After we are saved, redeemed, and regenerated to be saints, the Spirit lives in us. Every day the indwelling Spirit works not to correct us, change us, or adjust us, but to transform us metabolically with some element, some new factor, added into our being. Every day, without our being conscious of it, the indwelling Spirit adds the new element of God into our being, and with this new element, which is divine and is even God Himself, He transforms us metabolically. For many years nearly every day I have had the feeling that the Transformer is within me. The indwelling Spirit is transforming us.

On weekends many people like to pursue pleasures for their entertainment, but the saints in the churches are happy to use the weekends to attend conferences to hear the word of God from the Lord's ministry. This is a sign of transformation. It is not necessary for me to teach the brothers that they should love their wives and should not lose their temper toward their wives. I would rather tell the brothers that God is one with them and has even become them, making them God in His divine nature and life (but not in His Godhead). We are humans, but God is making us divine. This is wonderful.

In the New Jerusalem the precious stones are we plus the Spirit. The transforming Spirit becomes one with us, His transformed ones. Therefore, the pearls are Christ and we, and the wall of precious stones is the Spirit and we. These two items, the pearls and the precious stones, indicate that the Second of the Triune God and the Third of the Triune God have made Themselves one with us. Without the Spirit it would be impossible for us as pieces of clay to become jasper, bearing the same appearance as God. But now we have the life-giving Spirit, who is actually the consummated Triune God, in us, making us one with Him. Thus, we are altogether in the organic union with the Triune God.

The New Jerusalem is a city with three elements constituted into our being to make the Triune God mingled with us, His redeemed people. On the one hand, we can say that the holy city is just the Triune God. On the other hand, we can also say that the holy city is the Triune God mingled with all His redeemed.

The earth is not our everlasting dwelling place. As God's saved ones, we are sojourners on this earth (1 Pet. 2:11). We are traveling through to reach our destination. On the one hand we can say that the Triune God is our destination, and on the other hand we can say that the holy city is our destination. This is because eventually the Triune God becomes the factors of the holy city, and we also will be made factors of the holy city. The building up of the holy city is a mingling of the Triune God in His divinity with us in our humanity. The holy city is both divine and human. It is divinely human and humanly divine. There you can meet God, and there you can meet all the redeemed, including those of the Old Testament, who bear the label of the names of the twelve tribes, and those of the New Testament, who bear the label of the names of the twelve apostles. Such a city is both God and the redeemed. This is the structure of the New Jerusalem.

A Mutual Abode in the Organic Union

Revelation 21:3 tells us that such a New Jerusalem is first the tabernacle of our God, God's dwelling place for eternity. It also tells us that there is no temple in the city, but the Dweller, the Divine Trinity, who dwells in the tabernacle, is Himself the temple to be our dwelling place (v. 22). God dwells in us as the tabernacle, and we dwell in God as the temple. Therefore, we and God have a mutual abode (John 14:23). The New Jerusalem is God's home and also ours. We will be there to be His abode, and He will be there to be our dwelling place. This means that He will dwell in us and we will dwell in Him. He will abide in us and we will abide in Him. This mutual dwelling and abiding was spoken of by the Lord in John 15, where He said, "Abide in Me and I in you" (v. 4a). In theology this is called coinhering. We and God not only coexist but also coinhere. He exists in us and we exist in Him. Even a husband and a wife cannot coinhere. There is no possibility for them to abide in each other. But in the New Jerusalem there is the wonderful fact that God will abide in us and we will abide in Him, that is, that He and we will coinhere. This coinhering of God and us is an organic union. I believe that we will need eternity to show us what the organic union between God and us is. There we will realize and experience this union in full. He will abide in us and we will abide in Him. How marvelous this is!

Having God as Its Light and the Lamb as Its Lamp

Within the city there is God's throne, and God's throne refers to God's administration. God is the reigning God. He is the King, He is the Governor, and He is on the throne. However, this One who is on the throne is very peculiar. In Revelation 22:1 and 3 the throne is called "the throne of God and of the Lamb," indicating that there are two sitting on the same throne. These two do not sit side by side, but God the Father is within the Son, the Lamb. As the Lamb, the Son is a Man, the Redeemer, and the God who is within Him is the redeeming God. In Revelation 21:23 the Lamb is the lamp of the holy city, and God is the light within the lamp, shining to illuminate the city with the glory of God.

In this picture we can see three layers: the light, the lamp, and the city. God as the light shines in the Lamb as the lamp, and the lamp is in the city. Since the city is jasper, it is transparent (v. 11). There is no need of the sun nor of the moon to shine in the city, because God as the unique light shines from within Christ throughout the city to make the entire city a great lamp shining over all the nations around the New Jerusalem (vv. 23-24). All the nations will walk in the light of the city.

Again, in this picture we can see the organic union. In the holy city God and Christ are organically united, and They and we are also united as one. Therefore, there is an organic union between us and God and Christ. The entire New Jerusalem will be a great organic union.

The situation in the New Jerusalem is like that in the church today. God is the light within us, and we are the lamp shining out God. This means that we are shining out God through the church. Thus, the church is a big lampstand to shine forth the very Triune God as our testimony organically.

The River of Water of Life and the Tree of Life Maintaining the Organic Union

Not only so, out of the throne within the city flows a river of water of life (22:1). This river spirals down from the top of the city until it circles to reach the twelve gates. The water of life in this river quenches organically the thirst of God's redeemed (21:6; 22:17b; cf. John 4:14; 7:37-39). Along the river the tree of life grows as a vine (Rev. 22:2). This one tree growing on the two sides of the river is a spreading vine, bearing a new kind of fruit every month. That is, in twelve months twelve different kinds of fruit are borne.

The fruit borne by the tree of life is good for food (Gen. 2:9), good to nourish us. The water of life quenches our thirst, and the tree of life nourishes us, feeds us, and satisfies us organically (Rev. 22:14; 2:7). For eternity we will be in the New Jerusalem enjoying the Triune God, a God who flows out to reach us. By this we can see the Triune God: God as the light in the lamp is God the Father; the Lamb as the lamp is Christ, the Son; and the flow of the water of life is the Spirit. This is the Triune God flowing out of His throne to reach all His redeemed to maintain the organic union for eternity.

This is the end of the Bible, and this is the conclusion of the Bible. The Bible ends as it begins. It begins with the tree of life as the center, and it ends with the tree of life as the center, to carry out an organic union between God and us by our drinking of God as the water of life and our eating of Him as the tree of life. The water of life quenches our thirst from within, and the tree of life nourishes us also from within, by our drinking and by our eating. In the New Jerusalem this is not to produce the organic union but to maintain it. For eternity we will be organically united with God every day and every minute by our eating and drinking of Him.

THE NEW JERUSALEM BEING THE CONSUMMATION OF ALL THE WORKS OF GOD'S NEW CREATION OUT OF HIS OLD CREATION

The New Jerusalem is the consummation of all the works of God's new creation out of His old creation in all the dispensations through the ages, including the ages in the Old Testament and the ages in the New Testament.

In this universe God has two creations, the old creation and the new creation. The new creation is produced by God out of the old creation. First, we were born into the old creation, but one day we were regenerated to be made a part of the new creation (2 Cor. 5:17). The new creation is produced out of the old creation in four different ages.

The Ages in the Old Testament

The Age before the Law, from Adam to Moses

The first age was the age before the law, from Adam to Moses (Rom. 5:14a). In that age God remade many people out of the old creation into the new creation, including Abel, Enoch, Noah, and Abraham, Isaac, and Jacob. Eventually, they all became parts of the new creation.

The Age of the Law, from Moses to Christ's First Coming

The second age is the age of the law, from Moses to Christ's first coming (John 1:17). In this period God made many people of the old creation new. Moses, Joshua, Ruth, David, Isaiah, Jeremiah, and all the prophets were made new by God. They were made a part of the new creation out of the old creation.

The Ages in the New Testament

The Age of Grace, from Christ's First Coming to His Second Coming

The third age is the age of grace, from Christ's first coming to His second coming. This is the present age, the age in which we are today. In this age millions of people of the old creation have been made new. All the believers in Christ have become a new creation. We all are part of the new creation.

Actually, today we are both the old creation and the new creation. Whenever we lose our temper, we are surely the old creation. Whenever we walk according to the Spirit, we are the new creation. This can be illustrated by a butterfly emerging from its cocoon. While it is on the way out, it is part cocoon and part butterfly. In the church meetings we are all "butterflies," but after going back home, we may all go back to our "cocoon." Some saints may be ninety percent out of the cocoon and ten percent in the cocoon. Others may be vice versa. We are all in the process day by day. We are passing through a tunnel, a process in which we are being transformed out of the old and into the new. We are in transit from the old creation to the new creation.

The Age of the Kingdom, from Christ's Second Coming to the End of the Old Creation

The fourth age is the age of the kingdom, the millennium, from Christ's second coming to the end of the old creation (2 Pet. 3:10-12; Rev. 21:1). In this age God will finish His work of producing the new creation out of the old creation by perfecting those of His chosen people who were not perfected in the foregoing ages. At the end of the millennium the old heaven and the old earth will pass away through fire and be renewed to become the new heaven and new earth, into which the New Jerusalem will come to be God's eternal manifestation and expression.

THE NEW JERUSALEM BEING THE AGGREGATE OF GOD'S ORGANIC UNION AND MINGLING WITH HIS REDEEMED, REGENERATED, TRANSFORMED, AND GLORIFIED PEOPLE

The New Jerusalem is the aggregate, the totality, of God's organic union and mingling with His redeemed, regenerated, transformed, and glorified people. Thus, the New Jerusalem is actually a constitution, not an organization. It is a constitution constituted with both the Triune God and us, the redeemed people. This constitution is still going on and will go on until the day when we are raptured. At that time this constitution will be consummated. Then the New Jerusalem will come down as the final consummation of the church (Rev. 21:10). The church is the miniature of the New Jerusalem. We are now in the church to be processed into the new creation in full. In the New Jerusalem we will participate in the consummation of God's organic union and mingling with His redeemed, regenerated, transformed, and glorified people.

THE NEW JERUSALEM BEING GOD'S ULTIMATE ORGANISM

Today the church is God's organism, but on a small scale. Eventually, the New Jerusalem will come as the eternal consummation of the church to be God's ultimate organism. This organism is altogether an organic union, an organic mingling, of the Triune God with His redeemed people.

We are God's children. In fact, we do not need correction, nor do we need improvement or adjustment. What we need is transformation (Rom. 12:2; 2 Cor. 3:18). Transformation is our need. We are fallen people. Whether we are adjusted, improved, or corrected, we are still fallen people. We need to be transformed. In other words, we all need to be constituted with the Triune God as our divine element. Why do we still lose our temper? Because we are short of divinity; we are short of God. We need more of God. This is all that we need. By nature some of the saints are quick people. If they attempt to restrict themselves from losing their temper, they may lose it even more. The more we try to restrict our temper, the more we will lose it. The best way is to forget about our temper. The way of trying to restrict our temper is the way of the tree of knowledge of good and evil, the way of teaching, the way of the cultivation of morality, the way of religion. We should not take that way; we should take the way of the tree of life, the way of partaking of God as our life. We should forget about ourselves and our temper and only contact our God every day and every moment. This is why the Bible tells us to pray unceasingly (1 Thes. 5:17).

Anywhere and at any time we can pray, "O Lord, O Lord." Just by saying "O Lord," we receive some addition of God into our being. When we are in the office, we need not bother others by saying "O Lord" loudly. While we are doing our work, we can say softly, "O Lord, thank You that You are one with me." Just by saying this much, God is added into us. This addition of this divinity will transform us. Then, even if we try to lose our temper, we will have no temper to lose, because all our temper will be swallowed up by the addition of God. Our goal should not be to live a life without losing our temper; our goal should be to live a life that expresses

God. If people call us a good man, that belongs to the tree of knowledge of good and evil. We need to give people the impression that we are a God-man, even that we are genuinely God in His nature and in His life. They may say to us, "How good it is to have you in the office. When you are in the office, God is here." They may say this because we are among them living a life that is not a good life but a God life.

We should not try to adjust ourselves. When we try to adjust ourselves, we remain in the cocoon. We should not remain in the cocoon; we should be in God. The way to be in God is to turn to our spirit, and the way to make this turn is to say, "O Lord, Amen, Hallelujah." Just by saying this much, we are immediately in our spirit. When we are in our spirit, God is there, waiting for us. Then we enjoy God, we live God, and we express God. In a real sense, we even are God. If we all live a life that lives God, expresses God, and manifests God, what a benefit the entire human society will receive through us!

This is not a religion. The very dynamic salvation of God is the redeeming and living God. He has redeemed us, and now He is living in us and with us to cause us to live with Him in order that we may express Him. He is God in us to make us God in Him. We do not need to exercise our mind to think so much. We need only to say, "O God; O Lord; O Christ. Hallelujah, You are with me. I can live You, and I can be You." How simple and how wonderful this is!